# HUNTING DANGEROUS GAME

## TRUE TALES FROM AROUND THE WORLD

by

Vin T. Sparano

Skyhorse Publishing

Skyhorse Publishing books may be purchased in bulk at special discounts for sales promotion, corporate gifts, fund-raising, or educational purposes. Special editions can also be created to specifications. For details, contact the Special Sales Department, Skyhorse Publishing, 307 West 36th Street, 11th Floor, New York, NY 10018 or info@skyhorsepublishing.com.

Skyhorse® and Skyhorse Publishing® are registered trademarks of Skyhorse Publishing, Inc.®, a Delaware corporation.

Visit our website at www.skyhorsepublishing.com.

10 9 8 7 6 5 4 3 2 1

Library of Congress Cataloging-in-Publication Data is available on file.

Cover design by Tom Lau
Cover photo credit: Ken Laager

Print ISBN: 978-1-5107-1476-2
Ebook ISBN: 978-1-5107-1479-3

Printed in the United States of America

# CONTENTS

To my Grandsons Steven and Connor—
with the hope they will blaze new trails in their lives

# ABOUT THE AUTHOR

Vin T. Sparano has been an outdoor editor and writer for more than fifty years. He earned his B.S. degree in Journalism in 1960 from New York University. Sparano is Editor Emeritus of *Outdoor Life* magazine, having served as Editor-in-Chief from 1990-1995 and previously as the Executive Editor for more than ten years.

In addition to his long career with *Outdoor Life*, Vin's work in the field includes numerous articles and a syndicated feature writer for *USA Today* and *Gannett* Newspapers. He has written and edited eighteen books, including *Complete Outdoors Encyclopedia*, *Complete Guide to Fresh and Saltwater Fishing*, *Complete Guide to Camping and Wilderness Survival*, *Tales of Woods and Waters*, *The American Fisherman's Fresh and Saltwater Guide*, *The Greatest Hunting Stories Ever Told*, *Classic Hunting Tales*, the *Northeast* and *Southeast Guides to Saltwater Fishing and Boating*, *Hunting Dangerous Game*, and *Game Birds and Gun Dogs*.

Sparano's knowledge of hunting includes big game, upland game, small game, and waterfowl. His adventures have taken him caribou hunting in the Artic Circle and to Zimbabwe, Africa, where he has hunted dangerous game as well as plains game. In the United States and Canada, Sparano regularly hunts for elk, bear, antelope, turkey, mule deer, and whitetails.

Sparano is a familiar sight fishing from his boat, the *Betty Boop*. During the fall, his focus is on the great striped bass fishery off Barnegat Inlet. In the winter months, Sparano travels to Florida, where he fishes the famous Islamorada Flats for tarpon and bonefish as well as the offshore waters for sailfish, tuna, and other bluewater gamefish.

A certified NRA Rifle, Pistol, Shotgun and Hunter Safety Instructor, Sparano has been an active member of the Outdoor Writers Association of America for almost thirty years, fulfilling a term on its Board of Directors. He is a past President of the New York Metropolitan Outdoor Press Association and a Heritage Member of the Professional Outdoor Media Association. He is also on the Board of the Catch and Release Foundation and the Board of Governors of the Fishing Hall of Fame.

In 1996, Sparano was awarded the United States Department of the Interior Conservation Service Award by Secretary of the Interior Bruce Babbitt. In 2003, Sparano was the recipient of the Lifetime Achievement Award from the New York Metropolitan Outdoor Press Association for his extraordinary accomplishments and contributions to outdoor journalism. In 2009, Sparano was awarded a Lifetime Achievement Award from the Fisherman's Conservation Association. Sparano is listed in *Who's Who in America*. He lives in Waretown, New Jersey.

# INTRODUCTION TO THE NEW EDITION

As a young hunter, I encountered my first dangerous big-game when a black bear showed up at my deer stand. I didn't have a bear tag, but I'm not sure I wanted to shoot it anyway. The bear finally ambled off, but not before it made me a little nervous about the encounter. I had read too many stories in the pages of *Outdoor Life* of bears mauling hunters.

Eventually, when I became editor-in-chief of *Outdoor Life*, I searched out such stories. Why did readers love these hair-raising adventures? That's an easy question to answer: There isn't a hunter in the world who isn't intrigued about hunting an animal that can turn the tables and become the hunter.

Over the years, on many big-game hunts, especially with Jim Zumbo, former hunting editor of *Outdoor Life*, I thought I would never make it back home. It's these tough hunts that have found a place in my memory chest of adventures. But it was not until I hunted Cape buffalo in Zimbabwe, Africa, that I really faced the realization that I might not make it home. I think it was Robert Ruark who scared me before I actually landed in Africa.

Ruark's "Suicide Made Easy," the lead story in this book, was an adventure I read before going to Africa. Imagine my frame of mind after reading about Ruark's description of the Cape buffalo:

His horns are ideally adapted for hooking, and one hook can unzip a man from crotch to throat. He delights to dance upon the prone carcass of a victim, and the man who provides the platform is generally collected with a trowel, for the buffalo's death dance leaves little but shreds and bloody tatters.

That's exactly what went through my mind when Rob Martin, my professional hunter, said "We have a problem." Rob's words sounded calm, but they did not cover up a warning that my hunt could get very messy. This was not the way it was supposed to happen. I hit the Cape buffalo squarely in the chest with a .375 Holland & Holland, a cartridge the size of a banana. M'Bogo was supposed to go down. He didn't even flinch! In fact, the bull trotted off with his buddies.

Following that bull was not easy. We had to cross a bug-infested marsh with insects I've never seen swarming around my head and ankles. Temperatures were in the nineties, and there was no escape from the searing sun. When we got in range, I again hit the bull squarely in the chest with my .375. Almost defiantly, the bull trotted off again. What does it take to knock him down, I asked?

"That bull weighs more than 2,000 pounds and he's all muscle," said Rob. "You can't kill an animal like that with one shot. Even when you do kill him, the bull's brain never tells the body that it's dead."

We tracked that bull for another hour when we finally found it in some high grass. He suddenly showed up only fifteen yards away and glaring at me. "Shoot!" Rob shouted. "Quick now!" I put the crosshairs on the bull's chest and fired. This time the .375 knocked the buffalo off his feet and the bull went down. Had the bull dropped back because he was hurt bad, or did he drop back to wait for us to get with range of his horns and his hubcap-size hoofs? I'll never know for sure.

If you are trying to visualize the final shot that put my buffalo down, you have to look no further than the front cover painting on this book. The painting, by Ken Laager, illustrated the story of my buffalo hunt in the pages of *Outdoor Life*.

Make no mistake, you will experience fear when you face an animal that can hurt you and even kill you. Your mouth will run dry, your knees will feel weak and your hands will shake. I know because it happened to me.

In these pages, you will read true adventures of hunters who have faced grizzlies, leopards, elephants, man-eating lions, and rhinos.

Most hunters will never face such animals, but you can share with these authors the excitement of hunting dangerous big-game that will give you no quarter. I warn you. These tales may also make you very nervous next time you're alone in the deep woods.

—Vin T. Sparano
Editor Emeritus, *Outdoor Life*
Spring 2016

# FOREWORD

It was about 1966 when I first visited the OUTDOOR LIFE office in New York. I was enormously impressed, because I'd started reading the magazine in elementary school. Meeting the big shots who ran OUTDOOR LIFE was a heady experience; I compared myself to an aspiring actor walking into Hollywood's Universal Studios.

Vin Sparano was bent over a drawing board as I walked in. He was just a bit older than I, and I remember his smile put me at ease immediately. Perhaps New York editors weren't three-headed monsters carrying bullwhips after all. Vin's hospitality assured me that editors indeed were human beings.

As good fortune would have it, my relationship with OUTDOOR LIFE grew stronger, and in 1978 I went to work for the magazine as western editor. Early on, I realized that Vin was the adhesive that kept the magazine running smoothly.

About a decade ago, Vin and I made our first western hunt together. It was a backcountry elk hunt, deep in the Selway Wilderness. You might say the weather was inhospitable, as plenty of precipitation allowed us to thoroughly test our waterproof clothing. Despite nature's nasty performances, as well as some downright terrifying mountain trails, Vin never voiced his displeasure. The same smile that I'd remembered in New York years ago stayed with him, even though it was sometimes hard to see through a frozen, ice-coated mustache.

The hunt wasn't successful, but Vin was a determined man. Another elk hunt would be mandatory. It occurred a couple years after the Selway adventure, this time in Montana. Not only did the temperature fail to rise above 10 below zero during our entire hunt, but Vin scratched a cornea while riding horseback in the dark, and I sprained an ankle when my horse slipped and rolled on me. So much for Montana's elk.

On the plus side, all our hunts haven't been so unforgiving. One that SHOULD have was a far north adventure that seems funny now, but deadly serious when we were participating in it. Imagine crossing 80 miles of Arctic Ocean in a canoe, guided by an Inuit who hardly understood English, had no fear of the frigid ocean, and who would gleefully eat seagulls raw if required. Vin and I managed to live through that one, and I must admit it's the hunt I talk about most when tales around a campfire are in order. Not only did we survive it unscathed; we took home a couple of dandy caribou as well.

I could go on about plenty of other hunts, such as Vin's doubleheader on big Texas whitetails, and a couple of fine mulies and antelope in Wyoming. Suffice it to say he's my favorite hunting buddy, not only because he's excellent company and a good hunter, but because he's so well informed on many of the great hunts of times. It's always a pleasure to listen to him talk about them while we're in hunting camp. Vin has worked with thousands of authors and knows what it takes to make a good story. That's why this book is another of his superb works on the greatest stories ever written.

HUNTING DANGEROUS GAME is sure to keep you intrigued throughout, just as it did me. Leave it to Vin to come up with the best of the best.

I'm not surprised.

Jim Zumbo, Hunting Editor, OUTDOOR LIFE

# 1

# SUICIDE MADE EASY

## By Robert C. Ruark

*Robert C. Ruark was one of the first American writers to popularize African hunting adventures. Ruark's predecessors were the white hunters who also wrote of their tales in the African bush, but they were always brave, fearless hunters who became enormous security blankets for most of their clients in a tight spot.*

*Ruark, on the other hand, was not always fearless and he had no problem confessing this, especially when he hunted Cape buffalo. I've read all of Ruark's writings and it's obvious that he had a love, hate and fear relationship with buffalo. Ruark contends that hunting buffalo is like suicide because buffalo are always trying to kill you. After reading this tale, you may agree.*

**S**ome people are afraid of the dark. Other people fear airplanes, ghosts, their wives, death, illness, bosses, snakes or bugs. Each man has some private demon of fear that dwells within him. Sometimes he may spend a life without discovering that he is hagridden by fright--the kind that makes the hands sweat and the stomach writhe in real sickness. This fear numbs the brain and has a definite odor, easily detectable by dog and man alike. The odor of fear is the odor of the charnel house, and it cannot be hidden.

I love the dark. I am fond of airplanes. I have had a ghost for a friend. I am not henpecked by my wife. I was through a war and never fretted about getting killed. I pay small attention to illness, and have never feared an employer. I like snakes, and bugs don't bother me. But I have a fear, a constant, steady fear that still crowds into my dreams, a fear that makes me sweat Spanish fighting bull. I have killed Mbogo, and to date he has never got a horn into me, but the fear of him has never lessened with familiarity. He is just so damned big, and ugly, and ornery, and vicious, and surly, and cruel, and crafty. Especially when he's mad. And when he's hurt, he's always mad. And when he's mad, he wants to kill you. He is not satisfied with less. But such is his fascination that, once you've hunted him, you are dissatisfied with other game, up to and including elephants.

The Swahili language, which is the lingua franca of East Africa, is remarkably expressive in its naming of animals. No better word than simba for lion was ever constructed, not even by Edgar Rice Burroughs, Tarzan's daddy. You cannot beat tembo for elephant, nor can you improve on chui for leopard, nugu for baboon, fisi for hyena or punda for zebra. Faro is apt for rhinoceros, too, but none of the easy Swahili nomenclature packs the same descriptive punch as mbogo for a beast that will weigh over a ton, will take an 88 millimeter shell in his breadbasket and still toddle off, and that combines crafty guile with incredible speed, and vindictive anger with wide-eyed, skilled courage.

From a standpoint of senses, the African buffalo has no weak spot. He sees as well as he smells, and he hears as well as he sees, and he charges with his head up and his eye unblinking. He is as fast as an express train, and he can haul short and turn himself on a shilling. He has a tongue like a wood rasp and feet as big as knife-edged flat irons. His skull is armor-plated and his horns are either razor-sharp or splintered into horrid javelins. The boss of horn that covers his brain can induce hemorrhage by a butt. His horns are ideally adapted for hooking, and one hook can unzip a man from crotch to throat. He delights to dance upon the prone carcass of a victim, and the man who provides the platform is generally collected with a trowel, for the buffalo's death dance leaves little but shreds and bloody tatters.

I expect I have looked at several thousand buffalo at close range. I have stalked several hundred. I have been mixed up in a herd of two hundred or more, and stayed there quietly while the herd milled and fed around me. I have crawled after them, and dashed into their midst with a whoop and a holler, and looked at them from trees, and followed wounded bulls into the bush, and have killed a couple. But the terror never quit. The sweat never dried. The stench of abject fear never left me. And the fascination with him never left me. Toward the end of my first safari I was crawling more miles after Mbogo than I was walking after anything else--still scared stiff, but unable to quit. Most of the time I felt like a cowardly bullfighter with a hangover, but Mbogo beckoned me on like the sirens that seduced ships to founder on the rocks.

For this I blame my friend Harry Selby, a young professional buffalo--I mean hunter--who will never marry unless he can talk a comely cow mbogo into sharing his life. Selby is wedded to the buffalo, and when he cheats he cheats only with elephants. Four times, at last count, his true loves have come within a whisker of killing him, but he keeps up the courtship. It has been said of Selby that he is uninterested in anything that can't kill him right back. What is worse, he has succeeded in infecting most of his innocent charges with the same madness.

Selby claims that the buffalo is only a big, innocent kind of he-cow, with all the attributes of bossy, and has repeatedly demonstrated how a madman can stalk into the midst of a browsing herd and commune with several hundred black tank cars equipped with radar and heavy artillery on their heads without coming to harm. His chief delight is the stalk that leads him into this idyllic communion. If there are not at least three mountains, one river, a trackless swamp and a cane field between him and the quarry, he is sad for days. Harry does not believe that buffalo should be cheaply achieved.

Actually, if you just want to go out and shoot a buffalo, regardless of horn size, it is easy enough to get just any shot at close range. The only difficulty is in shooting straight enough, and/or often enough, to kill the animal swiftly, before it gets its second wind and runs off into the bush, there to become an almost impregnable killer. In Kenya and Tanganyika, in buffalo country, you may almost certainly run onto a sizable herd on any given day. I suppose by working at it I might have slain a couple of hundred in six weeks, game laws and inclination being equal.

As it was, I shot two--the second better than the first, and only for that reason. Before the first, and in between the first and second, we must have crawled up to several hundred for close-hand inspection. The answer is that a 42- or 43-inch bull today, while no candidate for Rowland Ward's records, is still a mighty scarce critter, and anything over 45 inches is one hell of a good bull. A fellow I know stalked some 60 lone bulls and herd bulls in the Masai country recently, and never topped his 43-incher.

But whether or not you shoot, the thrill of the stalk never lessens. With your glasses you will spot the long, low black shape of Mbogo on a hillside or working out of a forest into a swamp. At long distances he looks exactly like a great black worm on the hill. He grazes slowly, head down, and your job is simply--simply!--to come up on him, spot the good bull, if there is one in the herd, and then get close enough to shoot him dead. Anything over 30 yards is not a good safe range, because a heavy double--a .450 or .470--is not too accurate at more than 100 yards. Stalking the herd is easier than stalking the old and wary lone bull, which has been expelled from the flock by the young bloods, or stalking an old bull with an askari--a young bull that serves as stooge and bodyguard to the oldster. The young punk is usually well alerted while his hero feeds, and you cannot close the range satisfactorily without spooking the watchman.

It is nearly impossible to describe the tension of a buffalo stalk. For one thing, you are nearly always out of breath. For another, you never know whether you will be shooting until you are literally in the middle of the herd or within a hundred yards or so of the single O's or the small band. Buffalo have an annoying habit of always feeding with their heads behind another buffalo's rump, or of lying down in the mud and hiding their horns, or of straying off into eight-foot sword grass or cane in which all you can see are the egrets that roost on their backs.

A proper buffalo stalk is incomplete unless you wriggle on your belly through thorn bushes, shoving your gun ahead of you, or stagger crazily through marsh in water up to your rear end, sloshing and slipping and falling full length into the muck. Or scrambling up the sides of mountains, or squeezing through forests so thick that you part the trees ahead with your gun barrel.

There is no danger to the stalk itself. Not really. Of course, an old cow with a new calf may charge you and kill you. Or the buffs that can't see you or smell you, if you come upwind in high cover or thick bush, might accidentally stampede and mash you into the muck, only because they don't know you're there. Two or three hundred animals averaging 1,800 pounds apiece make a tidy stampede when they are running rump to rump and withers to withers. I was in one stampede that stopped short only because the grass thinned out, and in another that thoughtfully swerved a few feet and passed close aboard us. If the stampede doesn't swerve and doesn't stop, there is always an out. I asked Mr. Selby what the out was:

"Well," he replied, "the best thing to do is to shoot the nearest buffalo to you, and hope you kill it dead so that you can scramble up on top of it. The shots may split the stampede; and once they see you perched atop the dead buffalo they will sheer off and run around you."

I must confess I was thoroughly spooked on buffalo before I ever got to shoot one. I had heard a sufficiency of tall tales about the durability and viciousness of the beasts--tall tales, but all quite true. I had been indoctrinated in the buffalo hunter's fatalistic creed: Once you've wounded him, you must go after him. Once you're in the bush with him, he will wait and charge you. Once he's made his move, you cannot run, or hide, or climb a tree fast enough to get away from a red-eyed, rampaging monster with death in his heart and on his mind. You must stand and shoot it out with Mbogo, and unless you get him through the nose and into the brain, or in the eye and into the brain, or break his neck and smash his shoulder and rupture his heart as he comes, Mbogo will get you. Most charging buffalos are shot at a range of from 15 to three feet, and generally through the eye.

Also, we had stalked up to a lot of Mbogo before I ever found one good enough to shoot. We had broken in by stalking a herd that was feeding back into the forest in a marsh. Another herd, which had already fed into the bush and which we had not seen, had busted loose with an awful series of snorts and grunts and had passed within a few feet, making noises like a runaway regiment of heavy tanks. This spooked the herd we had in mind, and they took off in another direction, almost running us down. A mud-scabby buffalo at a few feet is a horrifying thing to see, I can assure you.

The next buff we stalked were a couple of old and wary loners, and we were practically riding them before we were able to discern that their horns were worn down and splintered from age and use and were worthless as trophies. This was the first time I stood up at a range of 25 yards and said "Shoo!" in a quavering voice. I didn't like the way either old boy looked at me before they shooed.

The next we stalked showed nothing worth shooting, and the next we stalked turned out to be two half-grown rhino in high grass. I was getting to the point where I hated to hear one of the gun bearers say, "Mbogo, Bwana," and point a knobby, lean finger at some flat black beetles on a mountainside nine miles away. I knew that Selby would say, "We'd best go and take a look-see," which meant three solid hours of fearful ducking behind bushes, crawling, cursing, sweating, stumbling, falling, getting up and staggering on to something I didn't want to play with in the first place. Or in the second place, or any place.

But one day we got a clear look at a couple of bulls--one big, heavily horned, prime old stud and a smaller askari, feeding on the lip of a thick thorn forest. They were feeding in the clear for a change, and they were nicely surrounded by high cane and a few scrub trees, which meant that we could make a fair crouching stalk by walking like question marks and dodging behind the odd bush. The going was miserable underfoot, with our legs sinking to the knees in ooze and our feet catching and tripping on the intertwined grasses, but the buff were only a few thousand yards away and the wind was right; so we kept plugging ahead.

"Let's go and collect him," said Mr. Selby, the mad gleam of the fanatic buff hunter coming into his mild brown eyes. "He looks like a nice one."

Off we zigged and zagged and blundered. My breath, from overexertion and sheer fright, was a sharp pain in my chest, and I was wheezing like an over extended pipe organ when we finally reached the rim of the high grass. We ducked low and snaked over behind the last bush between Mbogo and us. I panted. My belly was tied in small, tight knots, and a family of rats seemed to inhabit my clothes. I couldn't see either buffalo, but I heard a gusty snort and a rustle.

Selby turned his head and whispered: "We're too far, but the askari is suspicious. He's trying to lead the old boy away. You'd best get up and wallop him, because we aren't going to get any closer. Take him in the chest."

I lurched up and looked at Mbogo, and Mbogo looked at me. He was 50 to 60 yards off, his head low, his eyes staring right down my soul. He looked at me as if he hated my guts. He looked as if I had despoiled his fiancee, murdered his mother, and burned down his house. He looked at me as if I owed him money. I never saw such malevolence in the eyes of any animal or human being, before or since. So I shot him.

I was using a big double, a Westley-Richards .470. The gun went off. The buffalo went down. So did I. I had managed to loose off both barrels of this elephant gun, and the resulting concussion was roughly comparable to shooting a three-inch anti-aircraft gun off your shoulder. I was knocked as silly as a man can be knocked and still be semiconscious. I got up and stood there stupidly, with an empty gun in my hands, shaking my head. Somewhere away in Uganda I heard a gun go off and Mr. Selby's clear Oxonion tone came faintly.

"I do hope you don't mind," said he. "You knocked him over, but he got up again and took off for the bush. I thought I'd best break his back, although I'm certain you got his heart. It's just that it's dreadfully thick in there, and we'd no way of examining the wound to see whether you'd killed him. He's down, over there at the edge of the wood."

Mbogo was down, all right, his ugly head stretched out. He was lying sideways, a huge, mountainous hulk of muddy, tick-crawling, scabby-hided monster. There was a small hole just abaft his forequarters, about three inches from the top of his back--Mr. Selby's spine shot.

"You got him through the heart, all right," said Mr. Selby cheerfully. "Spine shot don't kill 'em. Load that cannon and pop him behind the boss in the back of his head. Knew a dead buffalo once that got up and killed the hunter."

I sighted on his neck and fired, and the great head dropped into the mud. I looked at him and shuddered. If anything, he looked meaner and bigger and tougher dead than alive.

"Not too bad a buff," Selby said. "Go forty-three, forty-four. Not apt to see a bigger one unless we're very lucky. Buff been picked over too much. He'd have been dead twenty yards inside the bush, but we didn't know that, did we? Kidogo! Adam! Taka head-skin!" he shouted to the gun bearers and sat down on the buffalo to light a cigarette. I was still shaking.

As I said, I was shooting a double-barreled Express rifle that fires a bullet as big as a banana. It is a 500-grain bullet powered by 75 grains of cordite. It had a striking force of 5,000 foot-pounds of energy. It had taken Mbogo in the chest. Its impact knocked him flat--2,500 pounds of muscle. Yet Mbogo had not known he was dead. He had gotten up and had romped off as blithely as if I had fired an air gun at his hawser-network of muscles, at his inch-thick hide that the natives use to make shields. What had stopped him was not the fatal shot at all, but Harry's back breaker.

"Fantastic beast," Selby murmured. "Stone-dead and didn't know it."

We stalked innumerable buffalo after that. I did not really snap out of the buffalo fog until we got back in Nairobi, to find that a friend, a professional hunter, had been badly gored twice and almost killed by a "dead" buffalo that soaked up a dozen slugs and then got up to catch another handful and still boil on to make a messy hash out of poor old Tony.

I am going back to Africa soon. I do not intend to shoot much. Certainly I will never kill another lion, nor do I intend to duplicate most of the trophies I acquired on the last one. But I will hunt Mbogo. In fear and trembling I will hunt Mbogo every time I see him, and I won't shoot him unless he is a mile bigger than the ones I've got. I will hate myself while I crawl and shake and tremble and sweat, but I will hunt him. Once you've got the buffalo fever, the rest of the stuff seems mighty small and awful tame. This is why the wife of my bosom considers her spouse to be a complete and utter damned fool, and she may very well be right.

# 2

# BEAR ATTACK!

## By Ed Wiseman, as told to Jim Zumbo

## Outdoor Life, January 1980

*What could be the worst nightmare for a hunter in bear country? The answer is easy. Bear Attack! Imagine an enraged grizzly tearing at your body with fangs and claws. There's no help within reach. What do you do? Play dead, like the experts say? Try to fight him off? That's impossible! Makes you wonder why you ever thought about big-game hunting in the first place. This never happens to golfers or tennis players, but then they never feel as alive as you do when you're hunting.*

*Ed Wiseman is a guide in the Rocky Mountains of Colorado. He knew what to do when a grizzly jumped him and began to maul his body. Wiseman had no other choice. But how does one fight off an enraged grizzly with a broken arrow shaft?*

The bear came at me with no warning. Ears flattened, neck hairs stiffly erect, it growled fiercely as it charged, full bore, right at me. I saw its flashing teeth as it came, and I knew in an instant it was a grizzly, although I'd never seen one in the wild before. There was no mistaking the hump on its back, the broad face and the guard hairs. I've seen a couple of hundred black bears in the woods, enough to know that this one was entirely different than the rest.

The grizzly's attack started about 30 yards away, and I had no time to raise my bow and arrow. For a brief moment I thought the bear would go around me. Maybe its charge was a bluff. I'd had close confrontations with black bears before, and even had them approach me, but they all eventually backed off, giving me nothing more than a good scare.

This bear kept coming, growling and snapping its teeth with each terrifying bound. When I realized it meant business, I shouted at the top of my lungs, but it was no use. In two more leaps, the bear would be all over me.

I'm 46, a full-time outfitter, and I make my living taking people hunting and fishing. I was raised in Colorado and live in Crestone, near Alamosa. Fourteen years ago, I decided to go into outfitting and I've been at it ever since. The country I hunt is one of the most remote regions in the Rocky Mountains of Colorado.

I had four elk hunters out that day, the last day of the 1979 bow season. The weather was balmy, with bright blue skies, and the warm temperature made for comfortable hunting, although it got chilly in the evening.

My hunters were W. C. Niederee and his son, Mike, from Great Bend, Kansas, and Rick Nelson and Jim Latin, both from McPherson, Kansas. On the last day, Ace Calloway guided Rick and Jim, Chuck Gibbs guided Dr. Niederee, and I took Mike. Al Brandenburg, my cook, remained in camp.

Dr. Niederee decided to hunt on a slope opposite camp that day. The rest of us rode out of camp together and split up about three miles down the trail. Ace, Rick and Jim rode south to hunt the East Fork of the Navajo River; Mike and I headed west for the Main Fork.

Mike was the only hunter in the party who hadn't seen elk that week. Everyone had seen plenty of animals, and Rick said he'd looked at about 85. I figured the Main Fork would be a good place to show elk because I knew of some pockets that were always good. The area was just off the Continental Divide; it was rugged country that few people penetrated. It was about 11 miles by trail from camp to the place I wanted to hunt, about five miles overland.

About two P.M. we tied our horses in the timber and began to hunt on foot. We split up and planned to meet at the other end of the meadows, where I'd intercept Mike. Although I carried my bow, I wasn't really hunting intently. I figured on looking for elk sign and later meeting Mike.

I worked my way along and kept my eyes open on some meadows in the timber. I thought I'd see Mike as he traveled through them.

He never appeared, so I wandered up toward the horses to see if he'd returned to meet me there. Freckles, my Appaloosa mare, and Buckshot, Mike's horse, stood quietly in the trees. Mike wasn't around.

I headed back down to look for more sign. We were in a small finger off the main ridge, and I knew there was a good chance that Mike and I would meet. About five o'clock, while walking across a small flat, I heard an ominous growl a short distance away.

For a moment, while the grizzly charged straight at me, I thought it might be trying to get around me. But I quickly discounted that possibility as the bear narrowed the distance to just a few yards, still coming full steam. At close range, I could easily see the hump on its back and the yellow guard hairs. The bear growled continuously, and its open mouth exposed a set of huge teeth. My shouts, which might have startled or turned another bear, had no effect. This grizzly was enraged, and I was in bad trouble.

The charge lasted only a few seconds. I was carrying my compound bow at my side, but there was no time to nock an arrow. My knife was in my day pack, well out of reach for the precious split second I had.

The bear was almost on top of me when I raised my bow, trying to fend off the attack. I shoved it in the grizzly's face, but it bowled me over. The bow clattered to the ground, and arrows scattered everywhere.

As soon as I hit the ground I curled up into a ball. I brought my knees up under my belly to protect my vitals, stuck my face into my chest as far as I could, and clasped both hands behind my head to cover my neck. My day pack was still on my back, and would offer some protection there. I had read many articles that said playing dead was the thing to do during a bear attack. I knew that no man is a physical match with an enraged bear.

The grizzly immediately started mauling my right leg with its teeth. I had little sensation of pain, but I vividly remember the sounds of flesh tearing as the bear ripped into me. As I lay there helplessly, my only hope was that the grizzly would tire of me and leave.

It kept biting and chewing at my leg, and I forced myself to lie as quietly as I could. I still felt that if I didn't present myself as a threat to the bear, it would quit and lumber off into the woods. Strange as it might seem, I never panicked, even as the grizzly continued to work over that right leg.

11

I felt the bear dragging me slightly, but most of the time it would bite into my leg, shake its head and bite into the leg again. It didn't use its huge claws, just its teeth.

Then the bear dropped my leg and bit into my right shoulder. It clamped down hard, and penetrated my flesh deeply with its powerful jaws. I didn't know it then, but the bear had bitten completely through my shoulder, from one side to the other. Later, at the hospital, doctors found puncture wounds all the way through. Clinical tests also showed it bit my shoulder twice, but there was no tearing, just deeply penetrating bites.

When the bear let go of my shoulder and started on my leg again, I remember telling myself this could be the end.

At that point I realized that this was more than a passing attack. Playing dead was getting me nowhere, so I desperately started thinking about fighting back. If the mauling kept up, the grizzly would surely kill me.

In the blur of the ordeal, I saw an arrow lying close by. I reached for it, and because of good luck or providence, it was pointing toward the bear.

I'm convinced that my hunting background was a factor that weighed heavily in my survival. I always trained myself to instinctively shoot at one part of an animal rather than the whole thing. I focused all my attention on the grizzly's frontal portion and brought the arrow up with as powerful a thrust as I could muster, all the while concentrating intently on a small spot that I judged to be vital. I'm right-handed, but the arrow was in my left. I plunged it deeply into the bear. Years ago, I was a meat cutter. I know something about animal anatomy, but lying on the ground with a bear tearing into me, I wasn't sure I could drive it away before it killed me. Survival was all I could think of then, and I knew I must try.

The arrow I used, a new Bear razorhead fitted on a magnum aluminum shaft, is one of the strongest made. Somehow, the arrow snapped in half after I drove it into the bear. I remember reading about people who have by some incredible force lifted wrecked cars off their loved ones; the human brain in such cases goes momentarily haywire and the adrenalin flows. Maybe that's what happened to me. All my senses were fine-tuned to driving off that grizzly. There was no other choice.

After the shaft broke, I reached for the arrow and yanked it back out of the grizzly. A stream of blood flowed from the wound, and I rammed the broken arrow back in again as hard as I could. I remember thinking that the blood looked like it was coming from the jugular. I was convinced I had struck a pretty good blow. At that point I thought, maybe I've got a chance.

The grizzly gave no indication of being hurt and kept biting and tearing at my leg. It kept on growling, just as it had done throughout the entire attack. Right after I stabbed it, it started on my left leg for the first time.

Suddenly, the bear stopped working me over and walked over the top of me. A great gush of blood from the bear's arrow wounds splashed over me as the animal stepped across. The grizzly loped off and stopped about 25 yards away. I saw it slowly lower itself to the ground. It lay still, and I knew it was dead.

I was off in a side finger of the drainage, and my only hope was to make it to the main trail where I might be found. I didn't realize it at the time, but Mike was only a couple of hundred yards away from me throughout the entire ordeal.

I got up slowly, unsure whether my mangled right leg could hold my weight. I tested it carefully and was relieved to find that I could walk. The main trail wasn't far, and I started for it standing up. The bleeding was starting to take its toll, though, and I felt myself going into shock.

I was about 90 yards from the scene of the attack when I heard Mike shout. I was surprised and relieved to hear him. I shouted back, and he appeared in the timber moments later.

Mike is 25 and a full-time farmer. He is tough and wiry, but when he walked out of the woods toward me, he looked like he'd seen a ghost. My physical appearance didn't help. I was covered with blood from the top of my head to the soles of my feet. Every square inch of my camouflage clothing was blood-soaked, and my face and hands were crimson.

Afterward, I learned that Mike had heard the bear growl as it charged me. He also heard my shouts. By the time he got to the scene, the attack was over, and all he could see was a great spot of blood-soaked ground, my bow and scattered arrows. He was convinced the bear had killed me and dragged me off. He moved slowly with a nocked arrow, figuring he'd be facing the bear too. Then he spotted the bear lying dead and realized I might be alive after all.

We used the limited supplies from a small first-aid kit to bandage my leg as well as we could, with strips of Mike's shirt for wrappings. I made myself as comfortable as possible, and Mike went for help. The sun was setting, and I knew I was in for a long, hard night.

By the time Mike returned with the horses, I was much weaker. He brought them over to where I lay, and they got jittery when they caught a whiff of the bear and the blood. Mike tied Buckshot by the reins, and when he led Freckles toward me, Buckshot reared back and shucked the bridle. The spooked horse took off.

Mike tried to position Freckles in a way that would be easiest for me to get aboard. But when I stood up, I lost consciousness. Mike eased me to the ground, and it was a while before I came to.

I tried a second time to get on the horse, with Mike pushing and lifting me. Freckles is a big horse, 17 hands high. That worked against me now. I got my foot into the stirrup, swung my mangled right leg over and grabbed the saddle horn. I talked to Freckles, who was still jittery, and she settled right down.

We started off, and Freckles got shaky again because of the strange smells. Mike was leading Freckles using only a lead rope and halter, so I told him to put the bridle back on. When he did, we had better control, and she calmed down some.

As we traveled, Mike led my horse, and he constantly looked back and said, "Ed, talk to me, talk to me." I was slumped over in the saddle, bent over to the front, to avoid passing out. If I tried to sit straight up, I'd feel myself getting dizzy and going under again. Mike tied my raincoat over the saddle horn to keep it from bouncing into my gut, but it was still painful to stay in the saddle. Riding wasn't helping my leg, which was still bleeding freely.

Mike wasn't sure of the country, and every once in a while, when my head cleared enough that I could look around, I'd give him directions to get us on the trail. I was having trouble maintaining full consciousness.

Finally we got to a large meadow, and I decided I could go no further. I knew it was foolhardy to continue because camp was still some 10 miles away and I'd never make it. The meadow would be a good place for a helicopter to land. It was about seven in the evening, and I knew I had to rest. I was the only one who knew where we were, and I had to get Mike ready for what was in store for him. I described the overland route to base camp. If he took the trail the way he had come, it would be an extra six miles, some of it with no visible trail. So he'd have to go across the mountains. It was the dark of the moon, and he had his work cut out for him.

Mike built a fire while I lay back and rested. He dragged wood to where I could reach it, but in his haste to get going for help, he didn't gather as much as I'd need. He piled the extra clothes on top of me. I told him to follow a nearby stream bed to a pond and then cross the Continental Divide. The ride downhill would be pretty steep going. But he'd come out about half a mile above camp.

I knew it was asking a lot of him to find camp during the blackness of the night, but I was confident that with the landmarks I'd described to guide him, along with trustworthy Freckles, he'd get there. All of my mountain horses are well oriented to the country, and they can find their way around as well as anyone.

After Mike left, I was as conservative as I could be with the firewood supply. As time wore on, thought, I knew I was going to run out. The closest wood was some distance away, so I tried to burn a somewhat green log that Mike had inadvertently dragged over.

It started to get colder, and I knew I'd have to do something for warmth. I saw the outline of a log up the hill behind me, and it appeared there was some firewood around it. I rested again, did some isometric exercises to stimulate body heat a little, and covered my head with a jacket to retain as much heat as I could.

There was no way I'd be able to get up the hill and return to the original campfire with wood, so I started dragging myself along the ground, hoping to start another fire at the log. I used both arms and my left leg, and every move was a painful effort. I kept my head as low as possible to avoid passing out.

It was only 20 feet or so to the log. It seemed 10 times that far, but I kept myself from panicking. I concentrated on little things-- like what I should do in the next hour, or two hours. I thought back about the sequence of events so far--I had survived a bear attack, my vital organs were intact, Mike was close by to assist me, I was at a point where I could be rescued, and now Mike was heading for help. It would work. Help could be on its way by midnight, just an hour or so away. Dr. Niederee would be there with medical supplies and I'd have my sleeping bag to warm up in.

But help didn't come by midnight. The evening began to pass more slowly, and I wondered if the men might be having trouble finding me. I was in an area where we seldom hunted, and no one in the camp was familiar with that part of the country.

A new problem came up. The evening breeze grew stronger, and I began shivering. I had to find protection from the wind, and looked about for some kind of shelter. I saw a small pine tree not far off. Its thick boughs grew to the ground. It was my only hope for a windbreak, so I inched over to it, covered myself with the clothing I had available and tried to get comfortable. I didn't want to sleep, because if I slowed my body processes, I would only hasten hypothermia. The combination of shock and loss of blood made it dangerous to risk sleep. I had no choice but to stay alert.

While I lay there, I assessed my plight. I'm a practicing emergency technician, and I know something about vital life signs. If I could withstand the loss of blood and shock, hypothermia would be the only thing that could write the final chapter. Curiously enough, I was confident that I'd survive.

Suddenly, I saw two flashlights above me, coming off the ridge. I yelled and heard Mike shout back. He was along, carrying a flashlight in each hand. It was about three in the morning. I'd been alone eight hours.

When he reached me, Mike immediately started a fire, but it was difficult because the wood was wet. Finally he got a good blaze going. I was eager for its warmth. He told me that his dad, Dr. Niederee, and Ace were on top of a high ridge. We spotted their flashlights, and they located us when they saw the fire. Mike hollered that he'd found me.

The position of their flashlights told me that they were too far down the canyon. They needed to go back to a patch of thick timber and then work their way down through it. Mike tried to warn them about a steep hillside near them, but they apparently didn't understand what he was saying.

About five A.M., Ace and Dr. Niederee appeared on foot, without medical supplies or sleeping bag. I learned that they had tried to work their way across some brush along the steep shale hillside when trouble began.

Ace's horse hit the shale, slipped and spun around. The doctor's horse, Puffer, slipped on the shale and slid about 10 feet down the mountain. Puffer somehow came to a stop, and Dr. Niederee eased out of the stirrups so as not to unbalance the horse. He got off, grabbed for a bush and fought his way up out of the loose shale. Puffer tried to get out but slid down another 100 feet. It was impossible for Ace and the doctor to get to the horse in the dark.

Later that morning some of my men tried to get Puffer out. They got the saddle, sleeping bag and medical supplies and planned to come back the next day with more help. But it was too late. In his attempt to get out, Puffer went over the edge of the cliff and fell 200 feet to his death.

Dr. Niederee looked my leg over and saw there was no immediate danger. He was concerned about hypothermia. The men built a fire to warm the length of my body.

After I was comfortable and somewhat warm, we spent the rest of the night waiting for the helicopter that was to come in at daybreak. Mike built a fire where he wanted the helicopter to land.

It began to get light, and we strained to hear the helicopter, but it didn't come. Time dragged because of the anticipation, and for the first time, I looked forward to going to the hospital.

About a half hour after daybreak the helicopter broke the Continental Divide, and we all heard it at the same time. It was a beautiful sound, and it didn't come any too soon. I was starting to shiver uncontrollably.

The Medivac team performed flawlessly and got me to Alamosa Community Hospital without a hitch. The pilot flabbergasted passers-by when he put the ship down smack in front of the emergency room door.

After the doctors looked me over, they quickly got me under an electric blanket. My temperature was down to 95 degrees, and my blood pressure was low. Dr. Niederee thought I'd lost as much as three pints of blood. My right leg from knee to ankle looked like hamburger. One of the small bones was broken, and there was infection as well as possible nerve damage. I also suffered bites on my left leg, both arms, and my right shoulder. I expect to go back in for surgery to help mend the broken bone in my leg, and some skin graft and nerve repair.

Now that the ordeal is over, I can't help but think back on incidents in my hunting territory. Once I guided a hunter who watched over a horse carcass as a bait. During the night, a bear dragged the horse, which weighed about 400 pounds, to an area about 100 yards away to feed on it. I assumed it was a big black, but now, I wonder if it could have been a grizzly.

About seven years ago, while I was away from my base camp, a bear moved in and destroyed it. I found seven-inch wide prints in the dirt. Again, I thought it was a big black bear.

Three of my clients have insisted that they've seen grizzlies. I know there are plenty of blacks in my territory; my hunters saw five during the 1979 elk bow season alone. The blacks are blond, brown, fire-engine red, black, and shades in between. I always figured those "grizzlies" were big blacks, but now I'm not so sure.

With the grizzly encounter now a matter of history, one of my most sincere hopes is that experiences like mine will not make people fear the outdoors. As always, any bear is to be respected for its potential danger, not feared. I don't know why the grizzly attacked me, but I have no qualms about going right back into that country as soon as I can. You can be sure of one thing, though. The next time I come across huge bear tracks, I'm going to wonder just what made them.

## Postscript--About The Man And The Grizzly

Ed Wiseman didn't survive the grizzly attack because of luck. He is a powerful man, and he was able to use his strength against the bear. He did not wish to kill the bear and tried to avoid taking an aggressive stand until he realized it was a matter of life or death. Since the incident, Wiseman has repeatedly stated that he does not want people to fear bears, only respect them.

Since the attack, biologists have learned that the grizzly that attacked Wiseman was an old sow, more than 20 years old and weighing about 400 pounds.

Until this attack, grizzlies were thought to be extinct in Colorado. Two were killed in 1951, before the bears were declared an endangered species. Both were about three years old. One of them was killed just a dozen miles or so from the place where Wiseman was attacked.

Wiseman owns Toneda Outfitters in Crestone, Colorado, and hunts year-round. He uses hounds for cougars and bears. Wiseman runs a clean camp, and wants only serious hunters. He doesn't allow alcoholic beverages, because he wants his hunters to be in their best physical shape each day in the mountains. Although he accommodates gun hunters, he is a bow hunter himself and specializes in archery hunts. He is an official measurer for the Pope and Young Club.

Mike Niederee, who was with Wiseman during the attack, says, "Ed is one of the finest outdoorsmen I've ever known. There's a local saying that nobody keeps up with Ed Wiseman in the woods. He's simply the toughest guy around."

One of his nephews sums up Wiseman's abilities this way: "Of course Uncle Ed won the bear fight. He wins every time."

# 3

# THE RHINOCEROS

## By Jack O'Connor

## Outdoor Life, January 1965

*Most hunters agree that a 4,000-pound rhino is stupid and shortsighted, but that's the problem. He's too stupid to be afraid, which means he will charge anything, including you, your safari car and even a school bus. A hunter can try to predict the movement of a cunning animal, but not with a rhino. No one can predict what he will do...and that makes him very dangerous.*

*The legendary Jack O'Connor writes about this armor-plated beast from the past and hunts where the dumb rhino has destroyed some pretty smart hunters.*

The rhinoceros is one of the world's largest land animals. The familiar black rhino weighs about 3,000 pounds, and its larger cousin, the "white" rhino, about 4,000 pounds. By comparison the big black African Cape buffalo weighs about 2,000 pounds, and the larger Asiatic gaur, (largest of the world's wild cattle) weighs around 2,700 pounds.

The rhino is one of the dumbest of all animals. It cannot get it through its pea-sized brain that it is not the cock of the walk as it was 50,000, 100,000, or 1,000,000 years ago. Yet it is a powerful animal, armored with heavy hide and a wicked lance on its nose.

19

For hundreds of thousands of years, the rhino had solved all difficulties by rushing at them and either tossing them or frightening them away. In Africa today, though a lion may pick off a rhino calf it if can do so with impunity, the lion wants no part of an adult animal. I am sure the larger cave lions and the sabertoothed tigers of Europe's Pleistocene felt the same way about the woolly rhinoceros of those distant days.

The rhino has a keen sense of smell and likewise hears very well. It is, however, extremely shortsighted and may see things only as vague shapes and shadows. Its bulk, strength and stupidity--combined with its curiosity and its habit of solving problems by running over them--make the rhino an exceedingly uncomfortable neighbor to have around. The animal is literally too stupid to be afraid. In the early days of the Uganda Railway that runs from Mombasa on the Kenya coast to Nairobi and on to Uganda, rhinos were very plentiful and it was common to have a rhino take on a train single-handed. The encounter sometimes actually derailed the small engines in use then. Often the rhino was killed, but sometimes it survived the encounter.

The rhino is a vanishing species and there are few in East Africa today where there were hundreds 50 years ago. Nevertheless, it is still common to hear rhinos charging four-wheel-drive hunting cars, trucks, or anything else that moves in rhino country.

In the summer of 1963, Prince Abdorreza Pahlavi, brother of the Shah of Iran, was hunting in Angola with Mario Marcelino, the white hunter who had steered my wife and me around the previous year. The prince and Mario were tooling around one morning through a section of the country where rhinos were often seen, when with no warning a rhino shot out of the bush and crashed into the front of the car, running its horn through the radiator and getting head and horn tangled up with the twisted metal of the car. As one could well imagine, the prince and Mario were a bit taken aback. How they managed to keep from being thrown from the car I have no idea. Anyway, they piled out shooting--and that was the end of the rhino.

It is quite common for hunters after game in the brush--a lion, elephant, kudu--to be charged by a rhino. Often the rhino is just coming up to investigate at a nice brisk trot, but sometimes it means business. I was once hunting oryx and lesser kudu in the thorny brush of Kenya's Northern Frontier District when I saw a rhino trotting upwind toward me, snorting like a steam-switch engine. My gunbearer and I stood still, but I was set to shoot or dodge, whichever seemed best. But when the rhino got about 30 yards from us it slowed down and apparently forgot what had riled it. The head went down, the eyes closed, and the rhino appeared to have fallen asleep. My gunbearer and I sneaked off and that was the last I ever saw of the animal.

The funniest rhino story I have ever heard was told me by my friend Robert Chatfield-Taylor. He was hunting elephants in the Northern Frontier when, just about dusk, the hunting car got stuck in the sands of a dry wash the Somalis call a lugger. The two gunbearers and the white hunter were trying to get it out and Bob was standing by when he heard a tremendous snorting and crashing of brush, and here came a rhino trotting up to investigate.

Startled half out of his wits, Bob rushed to the hunting car, and grabbed his double .470 to defend himself. The white hunter, who had enough troubles just then anyway, was furious. He grabbed a handful of sand, threw it in the rhino's eyes and shouted: "Bugger off, you bastard!" The rhino buggered off.

The rhino is a very ancient animal. In the incredibly remote Miocene and Pliocene, rhinos occupied both eastern and western hemispheres, and in the form of the now extinct woolly rhinoceros they ranged over Pleistocene Europe. Today they are found only in tropical Asia and Africa. The Indian form is now found only on the Assam plain. The "Javan" rhino inhabits Bengal, Burma, the Malay peninsula, Java, Sumatra and Borneo.

There are two species of rhino in Africa, the "black" and the "white." Actually, neither species is black or white--both are a dull gray. Rhinos, like hogs, like to roll in mud and dust--and often one sees red rhinos, white rhinos, blue rhinos, depending on the color of the mud they have wallowed in. A rhino I shot in Tanzania in 1953 looks in the movies I took to be so light gray as to be almost white.

The largest of the African rhinos is the square-lipped, or "white," rhino, which except for the elephant is the world's largest land mammal. It is called white because the early Dutch settlers referred to it as the wyt rhino, meaning the one with the wide square mouth, since wyt is the Afrikaans word for "wide." Because one type was called the white rhino, the other became the black rhino.

The black rhino is an odd enough animal, but the white rhino is such a strange-looking beast that it looks as if it belongs to another world and another era. The white differs in many ways from its black cousin. It has large, hairy ears, whereas those of the black rhino are round, small and naked. The white carries its tail looped over its back; the black holds its tail up in the air like a radio antenna. The white rhino is a grazer, the black is a browser. The white rhino is a much less nervous and irascible creature than the black.

The white rhino has longer horns than the black, and in both species the female has longer and more slender horns than the male. The record white rhino horn is a very old one from a beast shot in South Africa by Sir W. Gordon-Cumming, a British hunter, explorer and nobleman. It is 62 1/2 inches long and the rear horn is 22 1/4. The record black rhino horn is 53 1/2 inches long and is from Kenya.

There are two varieties of white rhino, the southern and the northern. The southern was at one time extremely common all over South Africa between the Orange River and the Zambezi. Many were killed by early settlers and hunters. By 1880 they were rare, and early in this century only about half a dozen remained in an isolated part of Zululand. A reserve was established for them. They slowly increased and now there may be about 500. The remaining northern white rhinos are scattered over a wide area in Uganda, Chad, the Central African Republic and the southern Sudan. The entire population of the northern white rhinos is now believed to be about 1,100.

There are more black rhinos than any other existing species of rhinoceros, but in most areas of Africa where they were once common they are now rare. My wife has made safaris in northern and southern Tanzania, in Mozambique and in Angola and she has never laid eyes on one. The only place I have ever seen more than one or two in a day was in the Northern Frontier District of Kenya. On a short safari in Angola in the late summer of 1962, I saw two rhinos, one with excellent horns. My wife had chosen to sleep in that morning. Later the big rhino was shot by another hunter.

The black rhino is a browser, not a grazer, and instead of having the wide square mouth of the white rhino it has a hooked, triangular upper lip. The point is prehensile, used to strip off the leaves and twigs the animals feed on.

The black rhino will stand around five feet high at the shoulder and weigh from 3,000 to 3,500 pounds. In spite of its great bulk it is light on its feet and a trotting rhino seems hardly to touch the ground. All rhinos carry a colony of half a dozen to a dozen tick birds, which I understand are a species of starling, around on their backs. The birds are supposed to make their living by eating the ticks from the rhino, for the folds of a rhino's skin, particularly around the lower parts, are generally crawling with ticks. The tick birds have better eyes than the rhino, and when they see something strange they fly chirping off their host's back. The rhino then charges around blowing and snorting and trying to catch the scent and locate the danger.

Old Faro, as the beast is called in Swahili, is found from Ethiopia to the Zambezi and westward to Chad, the Central African Republic, Nigeria and the Cameroons. At one time the rhino was commonly found in quite open country, and was likewise seen abroad at all hours of the day. When Theodore Roosevelt hunted in Kenya and Uganda in 1910, he saw and shot many rhinos in the open, white as well as black.

Today the rhino has been so harried that it is more generally found in heavy thorn brush, and if it is seen in the open it is generally at dawn and at dusk. In fact in many areas, stirring up a drowsy rhino is one of the hazards of hunting the beautiful greater kudu, as both species like dry thorny hills.

The rhino is a slow breeder. One calf is born at a time after an eight-and-a-half-month gestation period. The calf is suckled for two years and the cows do not breed oftener than every two or three years. It is common to see a cow rhino with a calf several years old and almost as large as she is. Where modern man with his rifle does not enter into the ecological picture the rhino can increase even with its slow rate of breeding and lack of intelligence because it is just about without natural enemies. But if the rhino is hunted much, its numbers go down because the species is slow to replace itself.

In some areas rhinos have been killed off to make room for native settlements. In his book "Hunter," J. A. Hunter, the Kenya white hunter, tells of having killed several hundred rhinos in an area where some Wakamba were to be settled and which was being cleared of brush. Many have been shot in the Rhodesias along with thousands of head of other game because of the theory that game carries the tsetse fly. Now these areas have no game but still have the tsetse fly.

Rhinos have decreased all over the world in modern times, however, because rhino horn is valuable, much more valuable pound for pound than ivory. And the reason that the horn is valuable is that the Chinese entertain the notion that it is a powerful aphrodisiac. The fact that the notion is completely without foundation does not keep the horn from being in great demand and fetching high prices. In East Africa, the horns of rhinos that have been poached are generally sold by African hunters to Indian traders and then smuggled out of the country on Arab dhows. The horn eventually reaches China. I understand that the way to use it is to cut a very thin sliver from the horn, powder it, and drink it in a hot cup of tea.

When rhinos were plentiful, they were slaughtered by the hundreds for their horns. In an old African book by Frederick Courtenay Selous, the explorer, museum collector and writer, I find the following: "One trader alone supplied 400 Matabili native hunters with guns and ammunition, and between 1880 and 1884 his store always contained piles of rhinoceros horns, although they were constantly being sold to traders and carried south. It sounded the death knell of white and black rhinoceros alike in all the country that came in reach of those Matabili hunters."

The fatal horn of the rhino is actually not horn at all but hair that grows together, and the "horns" are attached to the hide instead of the skull. Unlike true horns, they have no core. As we have seen, the record black rhino horn comes from Kenya and is 53 1/2 inches long with the second horn being 18 1/2 inches long. This is the only black rhino horn over 50 inches in the eleventh edition of "Records of Big Game," but 12 are 40 inches or over. Forty-four are over 30 inches in length.

Many excellent rhino trophies have been taken by Americans, several fine ones by hunters I know. Dean Witter, the San Francisco financier and widely experienced hunter, has taken two rhinos that went over 30 inches in Tanzania. Frank Hibben, the anthropologist and writer, has a rhino trophy with a front horn of 31 1/2 inches, and Elgin Gates took a 29 3/8-inch rhino in 1956. Boyd Williams of The Williams Gun Sight Company has a rhino trophy with a very long front horn. I have never measured it but I'd guess it to be around 30 inches.

The horns of the cow rhinos are longer but more slender than those of the bulls. Almost always the front horn is longer than the rear horn, but occasionally the rear horn will be as long or longer than the front one. Many people simply want to be able to say that they have shot a rhino, and consequently some pretty small rhino horns have been brought back from Africa and proudly mounted. I have seen them as short as eight inches. My one and only rhino trophy is nothing to write home about as the front horn is only a bit over 20 inches.

Just how dangerous is a rhino? As is the case with the rest of Africa's dangerous game animals, opinions differ with the experience of individual observers. Some men who have spent years back in the bush say they would hardly consider them dangerous at all--that to be hurt by a rhino a man would have to be either careless, unlucky, or stupid. One white hunter I know was run over, badly frightened, and terribly bruised by a rhino. He considers Old Faro the most dangerous animal in Africa because, he says, the rhino is the only African animal that will habitually attack unwounded. He says you can be tossed, trampled, gored or killed by a rhino you were not hunting and didn't even know was in the country.

In the old days of foot safaris, when white hunters and clients took out for the bush followed by long lines of porters carrying burdens on their heads, it was routine to have some ill-tempered old rhino come charging down to rout the porters, put them up trees, and scatter tents, chop boxes and camp furniture all over the countryside. In those days of many rhinos, those leading safaris always loaded their rifles, watched nervously, and hoped for the best whenever a rhino was sighted.

A rhino is a creature of habit. It generally waters between eight and nine o'clock at night and always comes and goes by the same path. Woe to the safari that unwittingly camps on a rhino's path. One chap I know had just got to sleep one moonlit night when he heard a mixture of snorts, grunts, shouts, yells. An instant later he was knocked out of his cot and his tent vanished as if my magic. He has a vague recollection of seeing his tent, loosely draped around a fleeing rhino, disappearing into the bush. The members of the safari were upset, but no one was hurt. Then and there they moved camp 100 yards out of the rhino trail.

Powerful rifles and full-metal-jacketed (solid) bullets are usually recommended for rhino. Thin-jacketed, high-velocity bullets would probably go to pieces pretty badly on the big, thick-skinned brutes, and most expanding bullets would probably give unsatisfactory penetration on his heavy shoulder blade. However, many rhinos have been killed with such mild rifles as the 7X57 Mauser, the 6.5mm Mannlicher-Schoenauer and the .303 British--

25

if round-nosed full-metal-jacketed bullets are used and the shots well placed. D.W.M. Bell, that great Scottish ivory hunter, killed many with the round-nosed solid military 7mm bullet.

Syd Downey says a rhino is easy to kill with a bullet through the lungs or with one that breaks both shoulders. An old-time South African hunter said a rhino went down within a few yards with a shot that went through both lungs, but that if only one lung were hit, it could travel a long way even though bleeding heavily at the nose and mouth.

My one and only rhino didn't appear to me to be hard to bring down. This animal had been shot in the guts with an arrow on which the poison was not very strong. This made the rhino sick and mean. It had chased and hurt several Africans, and when my safari went through the Tanzanian town of M'Bulu a game ranger asked us to knock it off.

When we found the rhino standing under a tree I would not have been more surprised and excited if it had been a dinosaur. I tried for a heart shot at 125 to 150 yards, but my rhino fever must have made me jerk the trigger, as the rhino ran off. I found out later that the 480-grain solid from the .450 Watts (wildcat predecessor of the .458 Winchester) had struck a bit low and behind the heart.

I had expected the rhino to come ranging down on me like an avenging spirit, stick its horn into my quivering abdomen and throw me over a thorn tree. Instead it whirled and ran like a rabbit.

Right then I really distinguished myself. I stopped my rifle's swing and the bullet went right past the rhino's ample fanny. Then mentally I gave myself a swift kick, swung well ahead of the fleeing rhino and fired with the rifle moving. I heard the bullet strike and saw the rhino stumble. When it had run about 50 yards it fell and was dead when we got to it.

That rhino that had to be shot might very well have died anyway, as it had a bad abdominal wound. Yet I felt strangely guilty for having shot this visitor from out of the mists of time. I'll never shoot another.

I have known people who have been mauled by lions and knew one hunter whom a lion killed. I have known several who have been mauled by leopards and tossed by elephants and buffaloes. But I have never known anyone who was badly hurt by a rhino, perhaps because there are not many rhinos anymore. Just the same, a rhino killed tough old Bwana Cottar, an American who was one of the best and bravest white hunters East Africa ever saw.

# 4

# THE LEOPARD

## By Jack O'Connor

## Outdoor Life, 1964

*It appears that the leopard is more objective about his victims than other dangerous animals. This cat doesn't care who he mauls. When I was a young editor at Outdoor Life, I would chat with Jack O'Connor for hours about his hunts in Africa. As he writes here, a lion or any other dangerous animal, for that matter, will pick a victim and usually stay with him...but not the leopard. If he is confronted by five people, he will try to chew up all five. He will turn into a buzzsaw, tearing up one, then another and another...until he is killed or decides to call it quits.*

*A big leopard may weigh 150 to 175 pounds, but he can still climb a tree and string up an antelope twice his weight. He's no pushover!*

The leopard is one of the handsomest of the great cats and in historic times it has certainly been the most widely distributed. With black rosettes on a golden body, the leopard makes such uniformly colored cats as the lion and the cougar seem drab by comparison. Some even consider the leopard more beautiful than the great tiger.

In recent times no other large cat has had anything like the enormous range of the leopard, and no other cat has clung to its range so tenaciously. There are leopards in the frozen subarctic forests of Siberia, in the bamboo and reed beds of China, over a large part of central Asia, in the Caucasus Mountains, in

Asia Minor, over most of Africa, all of India, in Java, Sumatra, on the Malay Peninsula, and on the island of Ceylon.

The leopard is still found over most of this vast range. But the range of the lion is constantly shrinking, and as game is killed off and jungle is cut down, the tiger is found in fewer and fewer places. Yet the cunning and furtive leopard manages to maintain its numbers remarkably well. Kill off the deer and wild pig on which the leopard preys, and cut down the jungle which shelters it, and the leopard will find a home in a little rocky hill next door to a village and live on scrubby chickens, village goats and dogs. Keep the goats locked up and the leopard will turn cattle killer.

The leopard is a gleaming, golden animal. In tropical areas its hair is short; in cold climates the pelage grows long in winter. In moist, dark forests, the coats of the leopards are darker--almost an orange. Melanism is not uncommon among the leopards of those areas, and now and then a black leopard turns up. These are often seen in zoos and are generally called black panthers, (in India leopards are more often called "panthers" than leopards). These handsome creatures do not belong to a separate race. Instead, a black leopard will show up in a litter of ordinary ones, just as a female black bear may have one black cub and one brown one.

In desert areas, leopards tend to be lighter in color. In 1958, when I was hunting in the southern part of the Sahara desert and in brush country that borders it, my companion, Elgin Gates, shot a very large and heavy leopard that was a pale buff, the lightest in color I have ever seen. The desert cheetahs we saw on that trip were even lighter in color, much lighter than the cheetahs of the high grasslands of East Africa.

The leopard is not a large animal. The big male leopard shot by Gates in Chad had then the second largest skull ever recorded and as leopards go it was an enormous animal; it went eight feet two inches between pegs, the proper way to measure all cats. In the then current edition of Rowland Ward's "Records of Big Game," the record leopard (before skinning) is listed as nine feet seven inches. I no more believe that record than I would believe the record of a man 15 feet tall. The notion of a leopard measuring between pegs the same as the largest lion is simply preposterous.

In fact, I cannot think of any more worthless piece of information for a record book than the length of an animal before skinning. Hunters will exaggerate just as handily as fishermen, and once an animal is skinned there is no way either to prove or to disprove his statements. Some of the "length before skinning" data on lions in the record book are equally preposterous. As is the case with American bears, the only measurements not open to chicanery are those of the skull.

Be that as it may, the usual safari leopard measures between pegs from five feet four inches to seven feet in length, and weighs from 60 to 125 or 130 pounds.

A. A. Dunbar Brander, author of "The Wild Animals of Central India," says the leopards that hang around villages picking up an occasional chicken or dog are much smaller and lighter than those that live in the jungle and devour deer and wild boar. The big jungle leopards, he writes, measure from seven feet two inches to seven feet nine inches. What he calls a "fair average specimen" measured seven feet five inches between pegs and weighed 152 pounds. This sounds like a pretty big leopard to me. I haven't weighed many leopards but I have weighed dozens of deer and can usually guess an animal's weight fairly well. I don't think I have even seen a leopard that would weigh much over 150 pounds. One I shot in 1959 in Tanzania probably measured about seven feet eight inches, as the hide made into a rug is now exactly eight feet long. This was a large, but not extraordinary male, solid and chunky, but I doubt if it weighed 150 pounds. I have heard of 185-pound leopards but they must be rare.

For its size the leopard is enormously strong. In East Africa, where there are many hyenas and where a pack of these strong-jawed scavengers will run a leopard off its kill, the spotted cat habitually hangs its kill in a tree, wedging the head into a fork made by two branches. It is not uncommon to see antelope and large zebra colts weighing twice as much as a large leopard hung up in a tree. One observer reports seeing a young giraffe that would weigh twice as much as the heaviest leopard neatly strung up.

I have never heard of a man-eating leopard in Africa, probably because wild game is plentiful and there is little incentive for the handsome cats to gnaw on human beings. In India, man-eaters are common and some of the most cunning and destructive of all man-eaters have been leopards. A leopard finally shot by the famous Colonel Jim Corbett, author of "Man Eaters of India," killed and ate 125 people between the time it started its grisly career in 1918 until it was finally shot in 1926. This deadly creature was a light-colored leopard with short, brittle hair. It measured between pegs seven feet six inches, and seven feet ten inches over curves. A rug of this hide would measure over 8 feet.

In India the leopard is a remorseless hunter of the monkeys, which are sacred to the Hindus and which are called langurs. The monkeys hate and fear leopards and scream at them whenever they are in sight. Every inhabitant of the jungle hates the leopard. The spotted deer (chital) bark at them and so do the little hog deer. When the large sambar see a tiger or a leopard they make a sound called "belling." It is possible to follow the progress of a tiger or a leopard through the jungle by listening to the racket made by the jungle folk.

In Africa, leopards are exceedingly fond of baboon meat, and the baboons hate them for it. On a couple of occasions I have seen leopards because baboons were making a racket. Baboons are courageous creatures and when the odds are on their side they do not hesitate to gang up on a leopard--and generally the leopard takes off while still in one piece.

All of the creatures of the jungle and the veldt are afraid of leopards and never fail to watch one when it is in sight. I have seen lions stroll through herds of feeding game. Individual animals would move off a little way to give the lions room, but otherwise they paid little attention to the great cats.

But when a leopard is in sight, everything watches it. Once in northeast Tanzania, Syd Downey, famous Kenya professional hunter, my wife, Eleanor, and I were scouting some new territory when we saw a herd of about 30 topis all gazing fixedly in one direction. We turned our attention in that direction and there, lit by the rays of the rising sun, was a gorgeous gold-and-black leopard standing against the dark-red stone toward the top of one of the little rocky hills called kopjes in Africa. I have never seen a more lovely sight. It was so perfectly staged that it seemed theatrical.

A leopard will prey on anything it can overpower, even creatures several times as large as it is. When I was hunting tigers in India, leopards killed two of our tiger baits, half-grown water buffalos that must have been three to five times as heavy as the leopard. In both India and Africa, leopards simply love domestic dogs, and many a beloved pet has been stolen by a leopard right out from under its master's nose. Mickey and Monique Micheletti, who outfitted me in the Chad in 1958, had a charming little mongrel bitch who used to awaken me at night by sticking her cold little nose in my hand. A leopard came right into the Micheletti yard on the outskirts of Fort Archambault and killed her.

In the wild parts of Africa, the leopard certainly has its place in the balance of nature. Wherever leopards are trapped out for their handsome hides, the baboons and warthogs increase, destroy the crops in the native and shambas, and often bring the tribesmen to the point of starvation. Along the Save River in Mozambique, where my wife and I hunted in 1962, the natives had just about exterminated both lions and leopards by building thorn fences around the waterholes and then putting heavy wire snares in the gaps so animals coming to water would be caught. Since a predator has to have water in order to digest meat, lions and leopards were more easily caught than the grass-eating antelope.

In the mountains of the Middle East, where it gets very cold and heavy snows often lie for weeks, the leopards prey on wild sheep, ibex, roe deer, their young on wild boar and Caspian red deer. They also pick up domestic sheep and goats, colts, village dogs. I have never gone out in Iran deliberately to hunt leopards, but in hunting sheep and ibex I have seen a surprising amount of leopard sign.

In 1959 I actually saw a leopard there. An Iranian nobleman named Yar Mohammed Shadloo and I had seen three handsome urial rams on a ridge across a wide draw. There was absolutely no way to stalk them, so the only thing we could do was to lie low and hope the rams would feed over to the other side of the ridge.

Presently they did so. My friend and I gave them time to settle down and also to come back for a peek over the ridge to make sure they weren't being followed--a wise but annoying precaution wild sheep often take. Then, fully expecting to find the rams as soon as we topped the ridge, we crossed the draw. But no rams did we see. Instead, we saw the signs that all three had left suddenly and in a hurry. Then we saw why. About 200 yards away and below us was the head of a juniper-filled draw and slipping through it we saw the gold-and-black body of a fine leopard. Yar Mohammed thought it would be worthwhile for him to go around and come into the draw from below on the chance that the leopard might still be there and emerge. But we never saw that handsome cat again.

The Uralian country on the border of Iran and Russia looks exactly like the rolling, juniper-covered hills and brakes of Wyoming, Colorado, Utah, New Mexico and Arizona. And like this country in the western United States, these Iranian mountains can get very cold with deep snow and driving, frigid winds. I had always thought of the leopard as an exotic, tropical animal, and seeing one in country just like our West gave me a feeling of overwhelming strangeness. It was as odd as if I had bumped into a giraffe when I was hunting pheasants in an Idaho stubblefield.

Ask any experienced African hunter which he considers the most dangerous African animal and he will answer right out of his own experience. If he has had a close one with a lion, the lion gets the vote. If he had been run over and hurt by a buffalo or tossed by an elephant, these are the creatures he nominates. Enough people have had close ones with leopards to hold them in great respect.

As a fellow with a tender regard for my own hide, I seldom take chances with dangerous game and try to never to shoot except when I know precisely where the bullet is going to land. I have, however, read everything I could find on dangerous game and I have talked to many white hunters who have had experience which cannot be duplicated in these days of less game and smaller bags. My own notion is that the lion is by far the most dangerous of the African animals, but the leopard if it were as large and as powerful as the lion would be much more dangerous.

A good big male lion will weigh around 400 pounds; an exceptional one may go 500. As we have seen, it takes a big leopard to weigh 150, and some weigh less than 100. A big lion, therefore, is around three times heavier than a big leopard and is, of course, enormously stronger. Anyone mauled by a lion is much more apt to stay mauled than if he had been worked over by a leopard. There are two reasons for this. First is the greater strength of the lion; second is the lion's greater tendency to stay with a victim. The lion that mauled my white-hunter friend John Kingsley-Heath so badly a few years ago stayed right with him and was oblivious of other people. On the other hand the leopard would leap from person to person, inflicting painful but not necessarily deadly wounds.

Powerful men have actually killed leopards (generally wounded) with their bare hands. A famous case was that of Carl Ackley, the taxidermist and sculptor who collected and mounted many of the animals in the Hall of African Mammals at the American Museum of Natural History in New York.

The leopard, a small female, sprang on Ackley, chewing and scratching him painfully. He grappled with it, kept its teeth away from his throat, managed to get it down, and crushed the life out of it with one knee by driving the ribs through its lungs.

I have been told that wounded leopards are even more apt to stand their ground and fight than lions. They are very fast, they are tricky, and unlike lions they do not reveal their presence by growling before they charge. Suddenly there is a snarling ball of black-and-yellow fury and all hell breaks loose.

One white hunter who was rather messily chewed was following a leopard wounded by a client. When the leopard charged, the client turned to run and got in the hunter's way so he was unable to shoot. The leopard knocked the hunter down and his rifle flew from his hands. The leopard then bounced from white hunter to gunbearer, then back to the white hunter, biting and clawing each. The second gunbearer ran the client down, took his rifle away from him, and returned to kill the leopard.

This white hunter was mauled quite severely. He had to go to a hospital, where he spent weeks in recovering. He did not, however, lose his nerve. Not long after he went back to work again, another client gut-shot a leopard and it was the white hunter's painful duty to follow it into a kopje where it had taken refuge in a crack between two great boulders. The white hunter followed up the wounded cat, and killed it with buckshot from a shotgun when it charged. Safaris out for leopards always carry shotguns for just such emergencies, incidentally, as a speeding leopard is much easier to hit with a shotgun than with a rifle.

A leopard story I'll never forget concerned the famous Bwana Cottar, an Oklahoman who moved to Kenya prior to World War I and made his living as a professional hunter and an ivory hunter. Cottar was rough and tough, a crack shot, and a giant of a man. He had many close calls and was mauled by leopards several times. He always said that somewhere in the bush there was a leopard who was going to kill him, but actually he was finally killed by a rhino.

A leopard mauling had left Cottar's left arm so stiff and crooked that it was almost useless for hunting and he had to do his shooting one-handed. Then one day he and a white hunter of my acquaintance went into some brush to knock off a leopard that had been wounded by a Kenya farmer. Cottar took the charge, but because of his bad arm he missed the shot. The leopard mauled him briefly and very painfully, then bounced off him to maul a gunbearer for a few seconds before it got away into another heavy patch of brush.

The sun was going down then and a storm was coming up. The other white hunter felt that it would be the better part of wisdom to leave the leopard alone for the night. It would probably stiffen up and might even die. No matter what it did, it would probably stay in that patch of heavy brush.

So the party, temporarily defeated, retreated to the farmhouse, which was not far away. Cottar's painful wounds were washed, disinfected and dressed, and Cottar began drinking whiskey to ease his pain. After dinner he was suffering so that he could not lie down and rest. Instead, the maimed and wounded old white hunter walked up and down on the veranda while the wind blew and the rain fell, taking an occasional shot of pain killer, and cursing every leopard that had ever lived.

As he drank and cursed he gradually worked himself up into such a rage that he could no longer stand it. He picked up a shotgun, hung a barn lantern on his crooked arm, and rushed out into the stormy night to settle accounts with the leopard. The wounded cat was still in its patch of brush, still full of bitter and defiant courage. Cottar induced it to charge and that time he didn't miss. He returned in triumph carrying his shotgun in one hand and the limp and rain-bedraggled leopard over his shoulder.

"By God," he told the other white hunter and the farmer when he awakened them. "I feel better now that I have settled scores with the blighter. A few more drinks and I'll be able to sleep!"

The first time I went on safari in Africa, I didn't buy a leopard license because it cost $75 and an official told me that I stood but one chance in 10 of seeing a leopard - pretty poor odds for my 75 bucks. Actually, I must have seen a dozen or more, several of which I could have shot. I saw my first leopard a half hour after leaving camp the first morning we hunted. One of the gunbearers whispered, "Chui," the Swahili word for leopard, and I saw the beautiful gold-and-black cat bounding across the fragrant grass for some brush.

Another time I had made a hike of about a mile just at dawn to take a look at a zebra a companion and his white hunter had put up as a lion bait. At that time my companion had shot a lion but I was still looking for one. When my white hunter and I got to the "hide" (the spot behind some bushes where the bait could be observed) a magnificent leopard was feeding on the bait and only about 80 yards away. I wished, of course, that I had bought a license but I had not and there was nothing I could do about it. Then two lionesses and three cubs showed up. They told the leopard what they thought of spotted cats in general and of it in particular and it had some appropriate remarks to make about lions. However, as the two lady lions moved in the leopard moved off.

In 1959, the first time I ever went all out to shoot a leopard, my wife, Eleanor, Syd Downey, and I went out the first afternoon to put up some leopard baits. Eleanor shot a zebra, her first head of African game. We cut it in half and hung the pieces in two trees about a mile apart. The next afternoon, we saw a nice big male leopard lying on a limb above one of the dangling baits. At the foot of the tree was a hungry male lion. Since it wouldn't be sporting to shoot a leopard marooned by a lion, we passed the leopard up and led the lion away from the bait tree with a freshly shot Grant's gazelle. But we never did get another leopard on that bait as a pride of lions insisted on hanging around and kept their smaller cousins away. We finally cut the bait down and let the lions have it.

The leopard is as much at home in trees as on the ground, and it can sleep in a tree with every evidence of sound and satisfactory slumber, quiet except for its long and writhing tail, which tells the quality of its dreams. Unlike most other animals, the leopard comes down a tree head first. Try that sometime when you don't have anything else to do.

In India, the shikaris (hunting parties) do not hang dead baits for leopards as they do in Africa. Instead, they stake out a bleating goat or a lonesome, howling dog, then either hide on a pile of rocks or in the brush or on a platform called a machan in a tree. In Iran, so far as I know, sitting up with a "calling" goat is the only method of leopard hunting ever used.

East Africa has the finest leopard hunters in the world. What I know about baiting for leopards I learned from a master--Syd Downey. Syd selects his bait trees with care. He likes to find a tree near a rocky kopje, where leopards like to den up. If the kopje is in good country and near open water it is almost certain to contain a leopard. He likes to have the tree so that the prevailing wind will blow in a direction that keeps human scent from blowing past the leopard on the route it is apt to follow. A leopard, incidentally, will seldom approach through a large open area. Instead it will come to a bait tree from the nearest brush. If it can find one it prefers a route along a line of bushes. A leopard is as silent as a shadow. One moment the tree is empty and nothing is moving except some vultures in a nearby tree and some buzzing bees on the bait. The next moment, there is the leopard, alert, beautiful, and terrible.

When Syd and I were hunting leopards, our "hide" by the tree where I finally shot mine was a pile of stones about 50 yards from the bait. We could squat behind them, and then when the leopard finally came, all I had to do was to stand up, put my left hand on the rock, rest the forend of the .375 against my hand, steady the crosswires in the scope against Old Chui, and gently squeeze the trigger. The leopard was quartering away from me and fell from the tree as inert as a bag of flour and never moved.

In more unsophisticated parts of Africa, leopards are generally shot simply when someone blunders into one, and the art of baiting is not understood. In Angola I saw some baits a Portuguese white hunter had hung. Nothing had been shot on them--and small wonder! They were out in the open--distant from water and from any place where a leopard would lie up. There was no concealed approach so a leopard would feel happy about sneaking up and looking the bait over unobserved. And the baits were so hung that the leopard would have no comfortable spot from which to feed.

In another area in Portuguese Africa, no white hunter had ever been able to bait a leopard and had no notion how it was done. A veteran East African white hunter came in, hung three baits, and shot three leopards off them in two days.

Brought to a bait either live or dead, a leopard usually affords a very easy shot and there is little excuse for missing or wounding one. However, there are several things to contend with. For one thing, the hunter must be still and remain quiet as the leopard has wonderful ears and eyes. For another, the hunter must keep his shirt on and not move into a position to shoot until the leopard is eating or looking in another direction. The hunter must also fight buck fever, a malady that is apt to attack almost anyone the first time he gets a good look at a wild leopard. Also, the leopard has an annoying habit of showing up when it is almost dark.

I shot my only leopard with a .275 Magnum, but I doubt a .375 kills leopard one bit deader than a rifle of a much lighter caliber. A skilled and experienced white hunter I know swears by a .243 Winchester with 100-grain bullets. Another has shot several with a .270 and 130-grain bullets and has never had a miscue. Yet another prefers a .30/06 with 180-grain soft-point bullets. Whatever the caliber used, the rifle should be equipped with a scope. My idea of the best scope for leopard shooting in poor light is about 2 1/2X or 3X with a coarse crosswire reticle. The shot can be well placed, even when it is too dark to see the intersection of the crosswires.

The leopard is a frail creature with delicate bones. It isn't hard to kill when hit right with a bullet that expands quickly against light resistance. But hit wrong, a leopard can be one of the most dangerous and vindictive animals in the world.

# 5

# BROWN BEAR--1962

## By Fred Bear

## Fred Bear's Field Notes,

## Doubleday, 1976

*Here are the day-by-day notes that Fred Bear wrote in his notebook in 1962, when he traveled with his bow to Alaska to hunt brown bear. The challenge proved one of the most dangerous of his career. Try to imagine driving an arrow into a giant brown bear at 20 feet! This is Fred Bear's amazing story. It's the ultimate challenge every bowhunter dreams about, but wonders if he's up to it.*

Friday, April 27--Aboard the "Valiant Maid." Bob Munger, my hunting companion; Ed Bilderback, skipper; Harley King, guide; Dan Korea, cook. Left Cordova, Alaska at 11:00 A.M. today. Went into Sheep Bay to check on bears. No sign anywhere. Will sleep here tonight.

Saturday, April 28--Came over past Montague Island and tied up at the cannery dock at Port Ashton. It rained this morning, but cleared into a fine day. Am concerned about the heavy snow still here. Most snow they have had in 20 years. The bears will sleep late this spring.

Sunday, April 29--Dropped anchor this evening in Nuka Bay after an eight-hour run from Port Ashton. Thought this might be a good place for black bear. We saw a coyote and some whales but no bear. Too much snow here too. We are early for bears. Heading for Afognak Island hoping it will be warmer there.

Monday, April 30--The weather was bad last evening. We dropped anchor for the night in Chugach Bay with its small coves and arms. Not so much snow here. Black bears in this area. We saw one in an open place on the side of the mountain. Went ashore and made a stalk, but the wind crossed us up. Took the skiff about five miles downshore and located another bear on a small beach, but he wandered off into the woods. When we saw a third bear on a beach nearby, we were almost within range when the wind changed and he made off.

Later, on another beach, we located more bears and circled through the woods until we were close. One of them came off the beach and bedded down about 20 yards from us. I shot some film of two on the beach. Later the one who had bedded down joined the others. They are digging kelp buried in the gravel. Bob shot an arrow at one and they scampered off into the woods. We scattered and sneaked after them through the spruce, trying to get within range. One had crossed a small frozen pond and I crossed after him. About halfway over I got an opening and shot the bear at about 25 yards. It was a lung shot and I kept after him. With my eyes on the bear, not looking where I was going, I walked into thin ice, and broke through to my hips. I found my bear a hundred yards away. We saw a total of six bears today.

Tuesday, May 1--We're anchored near an abandoned cannery in Graham Bay--too rough to cross to Barren Islands. Got here about 10:00 P.M. and immediately saw two black bears on the side of the mountain. We decided that Ed should show us how to do it this time. He started off with his bow and arrow. Grass very dry and noisy. The bear heard him and he got only a running shot. We did not see it again.

Did some scrounging around the cannery and an abandoned sawmill. Getting back to the "Valiant Maid" we found her listing badly. There had been a minus tide and she was on bottom. Tide came back and we were afloat again.

Wednesday, May 2--Made the first half of the run to Afognak. Threw anchor in a bay off an island this morning and got in the skiff to go seal hunting. We got a few nice skins. This country is covered with brant, yellowlegs, honkers, sandhill cranes, swans, all kinds of ducks, cormorants and gulls and terns by the millions. The wind is blowing a gale. Hope it calms down so we can move on to brown bear country. Wonderful weather all the time except for the wind.

Friday, May 4--Dropped anchor in Seal Bay on Afognak. Saw a bear near shore from the "Valiant Maid," but he saw us and made off over the mountain. We hunted all the bays in the area and at 8:00 P.M. saw two bears on a grassy hillside, but they also saw us.

We went after them. Ed and Bob went one way and Harley and I another. We climbed up beside a big spruce thicket and stood there about 10 minutes. A bear cracked some brush near us, but we did not see him. Had to leave then because of darkness. We saw two foxes and two otters and caught six king crabs in our trap. One crab measured 48 inches across.

Sunday, May 6--Continuing our search today we went down along the east side of Afognak to Isut Bay and saw a lone bear about three miles away in the hills but did not try for him.

We had a three-hour run back this evening and got here at seven-thirty. Going ashore we found that a bear had been combing the beach while we were gone. We plan to stay here now and hunt the area tomorrow.

Weather is beautiful. The reason we stay on at Afognak is that this definitely is a late spring. Afognak, being low country, is warm and we reason that the bears should be out here earlier. Kodiak Island is higher and has more snow. Two years ago, with an earlier spring, many bears were out there at this time. Had planned this hunt for the Alaska Peninsula, but that is closed for hunting this year from Puale Bay south.

Monday, May 7--Shot a sea lion this morning and a seal for bear bait. Placed them on different beaches and built a blind near each. A good way to photograph eagles and foxes also. We needed water and ran into Port Williams where we also stocked up on meat and groceries. We met a hunter from Flint, Michigan, and got some bear information from him. He said there was good bear hunting farther down the west side of Afognak. We decided to check it out and made a run into Big Bay. Took the skiff and ran over to a likely beach. As we rose to look over the bank above the beach, there was a bear just beyond, among the logs on the high-tide mark. We tried a stalk but the wind was wrong and he made off into the dense spruce. Checked several bays afoot and found many bear signs. This seems like the spot we have been looking for. As a matter of fact, it looks almost too good.

Tuesday, May 8--Went hunting afoot this morning. I got busy photographing some eagles and had to track Bob and Ed down. Finally found them and Bob had a big brownie dead on the beach. He shot him with a .375, but I did not hear the shot. Measurements will not be available until the head and feet are skinned. He has a monstrous head and should measure up well. There was another bear with the one Bob shot. Ed and I spent an hour looking for him, but no luck. Ed packed Bob's bearskin and headed back to the skiff. We weighed it when we got to the boat; 175 pounds. After a snack we went foot hunting again. Cut across land to some beaches. Back from the hunt at 8:00 P.M. I'm tired.

Wednesday, May 9--Went to look at the bear and seal carcasses to see if any bears were there. Cruised some beaches and came upon a medium-sized bear. Took some pictures of him and then decided to maneuver though the brush and try to get a shot at him with a blunt for pictures. The bear was about 30 yards out on the beach from us. As we were just about to come out of the spruce, somebody cracked a twig. The bear stood on his hind legs for a full 30 seconds. Bob had the camera and Ed was in front of me. I took the camera and started to run film as he made for the spruce to our right. He was huffing and puffing and I got some pictures of him before he was gone and I was out of film.

Thursday, May 10--Took the skiff and went out cruising the oceanside this morning. Saw one bear, but he heard the motor and ran off when we were half a mile away. Got back in at 3:00 P.M. Found two rubber crab-pot floats. This makes seven we have found on the beaches as well as a good supply of half-inch nylon rope. We do a lot of beachcombing when looking for bears.

Went out again at 6:00 P.M. Back at 10:00. Rained all day today, not hard, but steady. Located a bear at 8:30. He came toward us grubbing along the beach. We were hidden in the edge of the spruce. At 17 yards he turned broadside and I started my draw. He saw me out of the corner of his eye and made off. I got a bouncing-away shot at 40 yards. I was not too disappointed since he was rather small. We are well wet down tonight. Having the last two king crabs for dinner.

Friday, May 11, 6:00 A.M.--On our way back to the big bay we left a few days ago. Almost all tracks are headed south and that is easy to hunt on foot. We are leaving at this hour because we need high tide to get the big boat out of the bay. Rained all night and is still coming down. Fog settling in now.

I learned a lesson yesterday in my encounter with the brownie. I thought he would stare at me at least long enough for me to complete my draw, but the first slow movement and he was gone in a flash. He was 40 yards away before I could get the shot off, bounding like a rubber ball over the sharp rocks.

Those smaller bears move like lightning. He ran into Bob and Harley who were waiting up the beach, turned and came straight back past the place we had first seen him.

The bears are not eating grass. Those we have seen are eating sand fleas. These fleas are one half to three quarters of an inch long and look like a small shrimp. They live in about a foot of beach gravel. The bears lick fleas up so greedily that they swallow gravel along with them. The stomach of Bob's bear had a handful of rocks in it.

9:15 P.M.--Sitting in the galley. Dan and Ed are playing cribbage. It is getting dark and fog is settling in the bay. We are anchored near the mouth of a creek in Perenosa Bay. Bob and Harley went up the creek to see if they could catch some rainbow trout. Ed and I will go after them in a few minutes with the skiff. Saw a fox on the beach as we dropped anchor.

Saturday, May 12--Back at the bay where we placed seal bait. We had the seals wired to logs. Bears had broken the wire and carried them off. In late afternoon Ed and I were hunting beaches afoot and saw a bear. We hid in the edge of the spruce and waited as he slowly fed toward us. The wind was not exactly right, however, and he became suspicious and swerved off.

I photographed a silver, or cross, fox this evening and also a seal this afternoon. Start hunting at daylight in the morning.

Sunday, May 13--Went in to Tonki Bay with the big boat this morning. Located two bears on a beach. Got into the skiff, went ashore, and started the stalk. Almost overran them as they walked part way up the steep, grassy mountain that rose from the beach. Ed and I climbed to get above and ahead of them. Up to this point we had seen only a back or a patch of fur. We were carefully approaching the crest of a ridge when I saw a bear's head look over about 20 feet above us. At the same time I heard a snarl below me and there was a brownie prancing on his front feet and not liking the intrusion at all. I realized that it was a sow and the one above us a two-year-old. Fortunately the cub ran off and the sow was satisfied by his escape and also disappeared over the ridge.

Saw two more brownies on a hillside about two miles inland. Wind was wrong. May try for them in the morning. Caught some Dolly Varden trout for dinner. Clouding over and wind starting to blow.

Monday, May 14--A strong wind came up during the night, blowing directly into the bay where we were anchored. Pulled anchor in early morning and had a rough trip to the little harbor where we are anchored now. Ed pulled in alongside a small crab-fishing boat that was in here for the same reason--weather.

We planned to be on our way to Kodiak now to catch the early-morning plane, but weather will dictate the time. It has been raining hard all night. Got four king crabs from the fishermen and had a fine meal.

Guess I will have to call this hunt a blank. I have been within 30 yards of four bears. One of them 15 feet. Something always seemed to go wrong. None of them were monsters. Saw a great many Afognak elk yesterday. Some of them down close to the beach. Ed stalked some and shot blunts at them. Have picked up many shed horns.

10:30 P.M.--Still confined to our little harbor. Still raining hard, although the wind has let up somewhat. If it does not get worse we will make a run for Kodiak early in the morning. A lazy day. Have everything packed. Wrote cards, took a nap, and ate the day out.

Tuesday, May 15, 9:00 P.M.--Up at 3:00 A.M. this morning. Weather better so we pulled anchor and headed for Kodiak. Got here at 9:00 A.M. and tied up at the dock. We all had showers in a barbershop. Did some shopping.

I called home to see if I was needed and got orders to stay until I got a bear. Ed will give me a few days bear hunting in between seal hunts and I have good hopes of getting a brownie. Bob left at 5:30 tonight for home.

We will be here tomorrow for some repairs on the boat. May leave in the afternoon--if not, on Thursday morning.

Thursday, May 17--Left the city of Kodiak at 4:00 P.M. heading northeast on the outside of Marmot Island. Ten thousand seals were reported here, but they turned out to be 5,000 sea lions. Several beaches are covered solid with them.

Am sitting topside in a bright sun. Not a cloud in the sky. There is a slight breeze blowing and some rather heavy swells running. At 8:30 we are rounding the north tip of Marmot to the mainland of Afognak to search the shores for bear. We will hunt north of where we were last Monday.

1:00 P.M.--Checked a whale that had washed up on the outside beach of Marmot Island. Apparently it went ashore last winter. Got some handsome ivory teeth from the jaw and pondered over the scrimshaw work done by becalmed sailors at sea in days gone by.

9:00 P.M.--Anchored in Seal Bay, really a part of Tonki Bay. The weather was closing in with an offshore wind and cloudy sky. Bow in hand, I walked the beach for a while. On the open beach ahead a dark object was identified as a bear. Our plan was to circle through the spruce and come out on the beach where the bear was.

He was about 200 yards away, digging sand fleas and not greatly concerned about anything else since he rarely looked up. It was not possible to make the approach through the spruce as a cliff broke off between us. However, some large rocks furnished cover for the first hundred yards, and a few smaller ones from there on.

Ed had forgotten his .375 backing gun but had his .22 Hornet seal gun. Harley had nothing. I had my bow and a .44 Magnum. The question was, who was backing whom, and with what?

We took our hip boots off and made the stalk in stocking feet. There was a small rock near the bear that hid his head from us when it was down after the sand fleas. Almost no cover between us otherwise. Fortunately he was busy pawing among the kelp. Only once did he look up. We happened to be motionless at that time and he went right back to his meal.

We finally reached a point 30 yards from him that seemed to be the spot for action. Between us was noisy, loose gravel. The bear was broadside, but facing me slightly. His front leg was slightly back covering part of his chest. One more move and he would be in position for my favorite rib-lung shot.

The move turned out to be a look to scan the beach and there we were. Brownie ran off with much woofing and did not show up again.

Friday, May 18, 3:00 P.M.--Stopped at Port Williams and deposited some mail. Anchored in Big Bay now. Ed is changing oil and filters.

8:00 P.M.--Just came back from hunting the beaches that were so productive a week ago. Not any tracks since we left here. Plan to leave for the Alaska Peninsula at 3:00 A.M. tomorrow. Got some T-bone steaks and some Dungeness crabs at the cannery at Port Williams.

Saturday, May 19, 7:00 P.M.--Made a start for the Peninsula at 2:30 this morning. A southwestern wind made it impossible. Came back to Big Bay and are anchored peacefully here in the sun. Boating, like flying, is unpredictable. Plans can be made, but it is not always possible to follow them through.

9:00 P.M.--After the wind eased up we left Big Bay, came south, and went along the west side of Afognak to Paramanof Bay. Anchored in a small bay out of the wind about 200 yards off a small beach.

We were having coffee and cookies before leaving for a hunt in the skiff when I looked out the galley window to see a bear walking across the beach. He went into some alders that came down along one side of a creek. We rowed over, made a stalk, but the wind was wrong and he sneaked over the mountain through a draw. He was not a big bear.

We did some miles in the skiff. Examined beaches and found but few tracks. Went into a bay that drains an inland lake. Saw Dungeness crabs on the bottom in water five to eight feet deep. Speared a dozen with the long-handled spring gaff. Plan to go up this creek at daylight in the morning. There could be bears in the meadows surrounding this lake.

Sunday, May 20, 5:00 P.M.--Up at 6:00 P.M. Hunted with the skiff until 2:30, but did not see a bear. Went around Ban Island and dug some littleneck clams. Saw and photographed two foxes. These are not good beaches for bear. No kelp. There seems to be no waterfowl either.

Left Paramanof Bay and just got here to Malina Bay. Saw a single bear and a sow and cub high on the mountain as we came in. They made off as soon as they saw the boat. Planned to go ashore and hike in to

Afognak Lake. Just got our gear on when the rain started. Decided to steam the clams instead.

Flowers are beginning to bloom and the brown hillsides are dappled with light green.

9:30 P.M.--Ate a mess of clams and then hiked over the rise toward Lake Afognak. Did not get to the lake, but looked over a little country. Very little bear sign, but quite a lot of elk activity, although we did not see any. Took the skiff and hunted down toward the end of the bay. Bad wind came up and we turned back. Finished up the littleneck clams. Very delicious. Cloudy all day and cold. Rain off and on. Tops of the hills have been in the clouds all day.

Monday, May 21, 8:00 A.M.--Rain and strong wind all night. Everybody slept in. Our generator quit working several days ago, delaying our move to the Peninsula. Voltage has dropped and we are now lifting anchor to run around the corner to a cannery in Raspberry Straits. Rain has let up but the wind is still blowing. Everything lashed down for the trip, although we will be on the lee side of the blow.

Ed climbed a cliff along a beach yesterday and was amusing himself rolling rocks down on the beach. Harley and I were on the beach appraising the results when the larger ones fell on logs. A big rock weighing five or six tons perched precariously near the edge was finally toppled over and came down thundering with ear-splitting pandemonium as it crashed into the logs. Ed later told us of his efforts in dislodging this big rock. He put his feet on the rock and his shoulder against the bank and "gave it everything I had." He felt it move slightly and then "gave it a little bit more" and down it came. He didn't explain where "the little bit more" came from.

These rocks are hard on arrows. I have gone through two dozen blunts on this trip and have just six broadheads left. My bow is holding up well and so is the eight-arrow quiver. This has been a rugged test for it.

Yesterday we found a skiff pulled up on shore beside a Fish and Wildlife shack. Bear hunters had been there. We found a freshly killed bear skull, a fox carcass, and a skinned seal. This is the first evidence of humans we have seen on this hunt. Not even an old tin can or the remains of a campsite. Found a wrecked fishing boat on the beach in Malina Bay.

3:00 P.M.--Tied up at a cannery having their electrician repair the generator. A short in the brush holder. It was a good idea to take it out of the boat. It definitely needed a cleaning job if nothing else. Raining and still blowing. Very cooperative people at the cannery. I left my films there for them to run tonight. They will forward them to Kodiak for me. Left the cannery at 6:00 P.M. and dropped anchor here in a small bay. Hiked through a valley up a creek, but no bear signs. Plan to leave here at 3:00 A.M. in the morning.

Tuesday, May 22, 6:00 A.M.--Heard Ed start the engine at 4:00 A.M. Got up at five when the boat started to roll. We are headed for the Alaska Peninsula. We were wrong in believing it is closed to hunting. I did not know last night if we would go this way or to Kodiak. If to Kodiak, I would admit defeat and go back home. Dan has not been feeling well (the cook) and would like to get off the boat, but Ed is about as bullheaded as I am and he is the boss and we are heading for the Peninsula.

This surely stretches out this hunt and were it not for needing pictures I could have taken Dan's side and we probably would be heading for Kodiak. If I can get pictures of taking a bear, this will make the finest film in our company library and I am pushing my luck to this end. Still overcast.

10:00 P.M.--Just got back from hunting with the skiff. Got here to Alinchak Bay at 9:30. Saw a sow and two cubs on the beach. Would have stopped for pictures, but it was raining. It has been raining almost all day. Chilly, too. There is snow on the hills. Saw no bears from the skiff.

Wednesday, May 23--On our way with the "Maid" southwest. Not enough bear sign here. Going back to where we saw the bears coming in. It is still heavily clouded over and some fog, but no rain.

9:00 P.M.--Ran in to Puale Bay early this morning. This is where I killed the big brownie two years ago. Hunted by skiff and found the tracks of a medium-sized bear in a mud flat. It was fairly fresh as the tide had been out only a few hours. Failed to find him, however. Cooked up a mulligan and planned to hunt bears between four and dark.

Had an hour of sunshine this morning, but later we had rain and at four o'clock the wind started blowing the raindrops horizontally and we could not go out. Two crab boats came in here out of the storm and one anchored beside us. I took a nap, drank a lot of coffee, and dried my gear. Everything is a wet down.

Keeping camera, gear, and feathers dry is a serious problem. Cameras are carried in my backpack, which is not entirely waterproof. Have a heavy rubber pouch that I chuck the whole business in and tie it tight. Have to keep a plastic bag over the feathers of my arrows, even in fair weather, to protect them from spray.

Thursday, May 24--Did a skiff hunt for four hours, but saw nothing. Had a lunch about 2:00 P.M. and then went bear hunting again. Got back at 8:00 P.M. Saw quite a few tracks, but no bears.

Our eating habits are very irregular. Governed by the tide and weather and not so much by the hour. Low tide is about the middle of the day now. Had a few hours of sunshine this morning and then rain again.

Friday, May 25--This was the big day. The sun was shining early and kept shining all day. It was a good day for bears, seals, king crabs, and pictures. This was perhaps the most thrilling day of my hunting career, and not without some humor too.

Our hunting day did not start early. The crab pot was lifted first to yield three fine king crabs. One average size and two monsters. Next we took the skiff into Bear Bay, a rocky, shallow site with a short beach about 300 yards long. As we rounded the point and the beach came into view, a fine bear chose this time to walk out of the alders into sight on the sand.

We were a good half mile away. The engine was quickly shut off while we studied the bear through glasses. He busied himself pawing and eating in the sand and kelp while Ed slowly and quietly rowed toward the rocky shore about 200 yards beyond the edge of the beach. If we could make this without being seen, we would be hidden by a small point that came between us and the bear.

Harley watched the bear with glasses to alert Ed to stop rowing when the bear looked our way. It was touch and go. Brownie would paw and eat and lie down intermittently. The warm sunshine on his heavy winter fur doubtless brought out sleepy dreams of great summer days ahead gorging on spawning salmon.

Before we reached shore he waded out into the ocean, rolled over on his back, and, with his head and four feet sticking out, enjoyed the luxury of a saltwater bath. The tide was out. The narrow rocky shore met the thick alders at the high-tide line. The mountain started up steeply from there.

While rowing across the bay I had shot some 16mm film of the bear. On shore Harley was to pinch-hit as photographer. I reasoned that he could cover our stalk from a point some distance from us and would need the telephoto lens. As it turned out, the 25mm would have been proper. Mounted underneath the movie camera lens, I have a 35mm sequence camera operated by a push button on the fore part of the gunstock mount. This camera, a Robot Royal, will expose 24 pictures on one wind at the press of the button. In this way with one operator, both still pictures and movies can be taken. The 50mm lens covers the same area as the 25mm movie.

Leaving the skiff, we made our way toward a point that would afford a view of the beach and the bear. Ed and I ahead and Harley with his .270 and the cameras about 25 yards behind. When we were some 50 yards from the skiff we saw the bear's blond ears coming toward us. The wind was right. We motioned Harley to squat and be still. Ahead of us, there was a heaven-sent big rock about four by four feet. Hunkering down we made our way to it. This was the only cover on this entire shore and we were lucky that it was placed so conveniently.

We both knelt down in the shadow of the rock, Ed a bit to my left and I on one knee with the arrow on the string. We kept our heads down, sure that he would pass on the ocean side, and waited in great anticipation (not to say, apprehension) for the appearance of this alder king.

He was a good-sized bear. We had concluded that while watching him, through glasses, crossing the bay. Up to now, however, our only close look at him had been his ears and there seemed to be quite a space between them.

All kinds of thoughts go through one's mind in suspense-filled moments like this. Would he bolt like the one did two weeks ago when he saw me slowly start to draw the arrow or would I have only a frontal shot when he saw us and stared in amazement? We had to stop about 10 feet from the rock because of some sticks that lay ahead. He would see us before he was even with the rock.

I was determined to place the Razorhead through the ribs close up to the shoulder. This would be a clean kill. There could be no excuses. I worried about the three strands of my bowstring that had chafed off on sharp barnacles as I got out of the skiff. Would it hold for this one shot?

We waited. Finally, he was in sight. Twenty-five feet away and coming closer. He turned toward us and looked us over, standing still. We remained as motionless and quiet as stumps and did not register in the bear's consciousness. We could almost see his mind working--"odd pieces of driftwood came in on the last tide. ..." (Stationary objects are not considered harmful by the animal kingdom.) He turned broadside and walked to pass us. The 65-pound Kodiak bow came back with the ease of a toy. He did not notice the movement. The Razorhead sank to the feathers near the front leg. The impact was considerable and as he roared and exploded down the shore straight toward Harley, we wondered what the outcome would be.

Harley, however, endowed with the tradition of good showmanship, stood his ground operating the camera until the bear began to fill the view and it seemed prudent to abandon the camera for the rifle. Cameras are delicate instruments and should be put down carefully. But life is precious. The open shore, between the steep alder-covered bank and the water, measured a scant 20 feet and Harley's position was squarely in the middle of it. The bear's direction of travel was also right down the middle.

In some alarm we saw Harley, legs and arms flailing the air, cameras in one hand, rifle in the other, trying to scurry up the slope to leave the open shore to the bear. Ed yelled in his booming voice, "Take pictures. I'm covering you."

At any rate, the bear passed him at full speed. A short way beyond it tried to climb into the alders, but could not make it and rolled back down the slope near the skiff. He was dead in less than a minute after he was hit. The arrow nicked a rib close to the front leg, passed through a lung, cut a heavy artery near the liver, went through the diaphragm, and just through the skin near the back ribs on the far side.

We took pictures and left him to go back to the "Valiant Maid" for a bite to eat. It was high tide when we got back and his feet were in the water. With ropes slung under him we were able to roll him into the skiff and winch him aboard for skinning on the aft deck.

With the carcass intact he tipped the scales at 810 pounds. The skin squared nine feet and the length and width of the skull measured 27 inches. Ed paced the distance of the shot at 20 feet. The bear ran 90 yards from where he was hit.

It has been a very busy day, a very exciting one, and gratifying. A bear at 20 feet looks big when one is down on his knees looking up. Again it was proved that an arrow in the right spot will do the job quickly and humanely, regardless of the size of the animal. This was a day when everything worked out just right. The sun was out all day and the bear did his part in coming to us. Actually, it would have been a difficult stalk if he had remained on the open beach.

It takes breaks like this to be successful with either the bow or the gun, except that with a bow the circumstances have to be more refined and the timing exact. This makes the fifth bear that we have been within 30 yards of. The other four times something went wrong. The range handicap of the bow is great, but the thrills of getting close to your target make up for it. A good-sized, bow-legged brownie strutting toward one at 25 feet is a thrill well worth the time and effort. It's a great privilege to match wits with a noble animal such as this that nature has so ably equipped to take care of itself.

Saturday, May 26--This was an easy day. Fleshing the bear skin. Cleaning the skull. Cleaning up in general. There was time to make a summary of brown bear hunting:

They have only two enemies. Man and larger brown bears. As a result, small bears are jittery and alert, always expecting a larger bear to pounce on them. The big ones are easier to stalk, having more self-confidence and an admirable cockiness that commands respect.

# 6

# IN THE LOUISIANA CANE-BRAKES

## by Theodore Roosevelt

*When Teddy Roosevelt wrote this story more than 80 years ago, he hunted with and talked about two men who would eventually grow in stature as bear hunters. It's certain that Roosevelt, at that time, had no idea that these two men, Ben Lilley and Holt Collier, would be recorded in the outdoor journals as men who would make their mark among bear hunters.*

*This is Roosevelt's tale of a hunting trip in Louisiana. There was no holding our late president back when he went hunting. On this trip he and his friends killed three bears, six deer, a wildcat, a turkey, a possum, and a dozen squirrels.*

*"We ate everything except the wildcat," said Teddy.*

In October, 1907, I spent a fortnight in the cane-brakes of northern Louisiana, my hosts being Messrs. John M. Parker and John A. McIlhenny. Surgeon-General Rixey, of the United States Navy, and Doctor Alexander Lambert were with me. I was especially anxious to kill a bear in these cane-brakes after the fashion of the old Southern planters, who for a century past have followed the bear with horse and hound and horn in Louisiana, Mississippi, and Arkansas.

Our first camp was on Tensas Bayou. This is in the heart of the great alluvial bottom-land created during the countless ages through which the mighty Mississippi has poured out of the heart of the continent. It is in the black belt of the South, in which the Negroes outnumber the whites four or five to one, the disproportion

49

in the region in which I was actually hunting being far greater. There is no richer soil in all the earth; and when, as will soon be the case, the chances of disaster from flood are over, I believe the whole land will be cultivated and densely peopled.

At present the possibility of such flood is a terrible deterrent to settlement, for when the Father of Waters breaks his boundaries he turns the country for a breadth of eighty miles into one broad river, the plantations throughout all this vast extent being from five to twenty feet under water. Cotton is the staple industry, corn also being grown, while there are a few rice-fields and occasional small patches of sugar-cane. The plantations are for the most part of large size and tilled by Negro tenants for the white owners. Conditions are still in some respects like those of the pioneer days. The magnificent forest growth which covers the land is of little value because of the difficulty in getting the trees to market, and the land is actually worth more after the timber has been removed than before. In consequence, the larger trees are often killed by girdling, where the work of felling them would entail disproportionate cost and labor. At dusk, with the sunset glimmering in the west, or in the brilliant moonlight, the cotton-fields have a strange spectral look, with the dead trees raising aloft their naked branches. The cotton-fields themselves, when the bolls burst open, seem almost as if whitened by snow; and the red and white flowers, interspersed among the burst-open pods, make the whole field beautiful. The rambling one-story houses, surrounded by outbuildings, have a picturesqueness all their own; their very looks betoken the lavish, whole-hearted, generous hospitality of the planters who dwell therein.

Beyond the end of cultivation towers the great forest. Wherever the water stands in pools, and by the edges of the lakes and bayous, the giant cypress loom aloft, rivaled in size by some of the red gums and white oaks. In stature, in towering majesty, they are unsurpassed by any trees of our Eastern forests; lordlier kings of the green-leaved world are not to be found until we reach the sequoias and redwoods of the Sierras. Among them grow many other trees- hackleberry, thorn, honey-locust, tupelo, pecan, and ash. In the cypress sloughs the singular knees of the trees stand two or three feet above the black ooze. Palmettos grow thickly in places. The cane-brakes stretch along the slight rises of ground, often extending for miles, forming one of the most striking and interesting features of the country. They choke out other growths, the feathery, graceful canes standing in ranks, tall, slender, serried, each but a few inches from his brother, and springing to a height of fifteen or twenty feet. They look like bamboos; they are well-nigh impenetrable to a man on horseback; even on foot they make difficult walking unless free use is made of the heavy bush-knife. It is impossible to see through them for more than fifteen or twenty paces, and often for not half that distance. Bears make their lairs in them, and they are the refuge for hunted things. In the swamp, bushes of many kinds grow thick among the tall trees, and vines and creepers climb the trunks and hang in trailing festoons from the branches. Here, likewise, the bush-knife is in constant play, as the skilled horsemen thread their way, often at a gallop , in and out among the great tree-trunks, and through the dense, tangled, thorny undergrowth.

In the lakes and larger bayous we saw alligators and garfish; and monstrous snapping turtles, fearsome brutes of the slime, as heavy as a man, with huge horny beaks that with a single snap could take off a man's hand or foot. One of the planters with us had lost part of his hand to an alligator; and had seen a companion seized by the foot by a huge garfish from which he was rescued with the utmost difficulty by his fellow swimmers. There were black bass in the water, too, and they gave us many a good meal. Thick-bodied water-moccasins, foul and dangerous, kept near the water; and farther back in the swamp we killed rattlesnakes and copperheads.

Coon and possum were very plentiful, and in the streams there were minks and a few otters. Black squirrels barked in the tops of the tall trees or descended to the ground to gather nuts or gnaw the shed deer-antlers-the latter a habit they shared with the wood-rats. To me the most interesting of the smaller mammals, however, were the swamp-rabbits, which were thoroughly amphibious in their habits, not only swimming but diving, and taking to the water almost as freely as if they were muskrats. They lived in the depths of the woods and beside the lonely bayous.

Birds were plentiful. Mocking-birds abounded in the clearings, where, among many sparrows of more common kind, I saw the painted finch, the gaudily colored brother of our little indigo-bunting, though at this season his plumage was faded and dim. In the thick woods where we hunted there were many cardinal-birds and winter wrens, both in full song. Thrashers were even more common; but so cautious that it was rather difficult to see them, in spite of their incessant clucking and calling and their occasional bursts of song. There were crowds of warblers and vireos of many different kinds, evidently migrants from the North, and generally silent. The most characteristic birds, however, were the woodpeckers, of which there were seven or eight species, the commonest around our camp being the handsome red-bellied, the brother of the redhead which we saw in the clearings. The most notable birds and those which most interested me were the great ivory-billed woodpeckers. Of these I saw three, all of them in groves of giant cypress; their brilliant white bills contrasted finely with the black of their general plumage. They were noisy but wary, and they seemed to me to set off the wildness of the swamp as much as any of the beasts of the chase. Among the birds of prey the commonest were the barred owls, which I have never elsewhere found so plentiful. Their hooting and yelling were heard all around us throughout the night. One of these owls had caught and was devouring a snake in the late afternoon, while it was still daylight. In the dark nights and still mornings and evenings their cries seemed strange and unearthly, the long hoots varied by screeches, and by all kinds of uncanny noises.

At our first camp our tents were pitched by the bayou. For four days the weather was hot, with steaming rains; after that it grew cool and clear. Huge biting flies, bigger than bees, attacked our horses, but the insect plagues, so veritable a scourge in this country during the months of warm weather, had well-nigh vanished in the first few weeks of the fall.

The morning after we reached camp we were joined by Ben Lilley, the hunter, a spare, full-bearded man, with mild, gentle, blue eyes and a frame of steel and whip-cord. I never met any other man so indifferent to fatigue and hardship. He equaled Cooper's Deerslayer in woodcraft, in hardihood, in simplicity - and also in loquacity. The morning he joined us in camp, he had come on foot through the thick woods, followed by his two dogs, and had neither eaten nor drunk for twenty-four hours; for he did not like to drink the swamp water. It had rained hard throughout the night and he had no shelter, no rubber coat, nothing but the clothes he was wearing, and the ground was too wet for him to lie on; so he perched in a crooked tree in the beating rain, much as if he had been a wild turkey. But he was not in the least tired when he struck camp; and, though he slept an hour after breakfast, it was chiefly because he had nothing else to do, inasmuch as it was Sunday, on which day he never hunted nor labored. He could run through the woods like a buck, was far more enduring, and quite as indifferent to weather, though he was over fifty years old. He had trapped and hunted throughout almost all the half-century of his life, and on trail of game he was as sure as his own hounds. His observations on wild creatures were singularly close and accurate. He was particularly fond of the chase of the bear, which he followed by himself, with one or two dogs; often he would be on the trail of his quarry for days at a time, lying down to sleep wherever night overtook him; and he had killed over a hundred and twenty bears.

Late in the evening of the same day we were joined by two gentlemen, to whom we owed the success of our hunt. They were Messrs. Clive and Harley Metcalf, planters from Mississippi, men in the prime of life, thorough woodsmen and hunters, skilled marksmen, and utterly fearless horsemen. For a quarter of a century they had hunted bear and deer with horse and hound, and were masters of the art. They brought with them their pack of bearhounds, only one, however, being a thoroughly stanch and seasoned veteran. The pack was under the immediate control of a Negro hunter, Holt Collier, in his own way as remarkable a character as Ben Lilley. He was a man of sixty and could neither read nor write, but he had all the dignity of an African chief, and for half a century he had been a bear-hunter, having killed or assisted in killing over three thousand bears. He had been born a slave on the Hinds plantation, his father, an old man when he was born, having been the body-servant and cook of "old General Hinds," as he called him, when the latter fought under Jackson at New Orleans. When ten years old Holt had been taken on the horse behind his young master, the Hinds of that day, on a bear-hunt, when he killed his first bear. In the Civil War he had not only followed his master to battle as his body-servant but had acted under him as sharpshooter against the Union soldiers. After the war he continued to stay with his master until the latter died, and had then been adopted by the Metcalfs; and he felt that he had brought them up, and treated them with that mixture of affection and grumbling respect which an old nurse shows toward the lad who has ceased being a child. The two Metcalfs and Holt understood one another thoroughly, and understood their hounds and the game their hounds followed almost as thoroughly.

They had killed many deer and wildcat, and now and then a panther; but their favorite game was the black bear, which, until within a very few years, was extraordinarily plentiful in the swamps and cane-brakes on both sides of the lower Mississippi, and which is still found here and there, although greatly diminished. In Louisiana and Mississippi the bears go into their dens toward the end of January, usually in hollow trees, often very high up in living trees, but often also in great logs that lie rotting on the ground. They come forth toward the end of April, the cubs having been born in the interval. At this time the bears are nearly as fat as when they enter their dens in January; but they lose their fat very rapidly. On first coming out in the spring they usually eat ash buds and the tender young cane called mutton-cane, and at that season they generally refuse to eat the acorns even when they are plentiful. According to my informants it is at this season that they are most apt to take to killing stock, almost always the hogs which run wild or semiwild in the woods. They are very individual in their habits, however; many of them never touch stock, while others, usually old he bears, may kill numbers of hogs; in one case an old he bear began this hog-killing just as soon as he left his den. In the summer months they find but little to eat, and it is at this season that they are most industrious in hunting for grubs, insects, frogs, and small mammals. In some neighborhoods they do not eat fish, while in other places, perhaps not far away, they not only greedily eat dead fish, but will themselves kill fish if they can find them in shallow pools left by the receding waters. As soon as the mast is on the ground they begin to feed upon it, and when the acorns and pecans are plentiful they eat nothing else, though at first berries and grapes are eaten also. When in November the have begun only to eat the acorns they put on fat as no other wild animal does, and by the end of December a full-grown bear may weigh at least twice as much as it does in August. Old he bears which in August weigh three hundred pounds and upward will toward the end of December weigh six hundred pounds, and even more in exceptional cases.

Bears vary greatly in their habits in different localities, in addition to the individual variation among those of the same neighborhood. Around Avery Island, John McIlhenny's plantation, the bears only appear from June to November; there they never kill hogs, but feed at first on corn and then on sugar-cane, doing immense damage in the fields, quite as much as hogs would do. But when we were on the Tensas we visited a family of settlers who lived right in the midst of the forest ten miles from any neighbors; and although bears were plentiful around them they never molested their corn-fields-in which the coons, however, did great damage.

A big bear is cunning, and a dangerous fighter to the dogs. It is only in exceptional cases, however, that these black bears, even when wounded and at bay, are dangerous to men. Each of the hunters with whom I was camped had been charged by one or two among the scores or hundreds of bears he had slain, but no one of them had ever been injured, although they knew other men who had been injured. Their immunity was due to their own skill and coolness; for when the dogs were around the bear the hunter invariably killed the bear at once to save the pack. Each of the Metcalfs had on one occasion killed a large bear with a knife, when the hounds had seized it and the man dared not fire for fear of shooting one of them. They had in their younger days hunted with a General Hamberlin, a Mississippi planter whom they well knew, who was then already an old man. He was passionately addicted to the chase of the bear, not only because of the sport it afforded, but also as a matter of vengeance; for his father, also a keen bearhunter, had been killed by a bear. It was an old he, which he had wounded and had been bayed by the dogs; it attacked him, biting him so severely that he died a couple of days later. This was in 1847. Mr. W.H. Lambeth sends the following account of the fatal encounter:

"I send you an extract from the 'Brother Jonathan,' published in New York in 1847:

" 'Dr. Monroe Hamberlin, Robert Wilson, Joe Brazeil, and others left Satartia, Miss., and in going up Big Sunflower River, met Mr. Leiser and his party of hunters returning to Vicksburg. Mr. Leiser told Dr. Hamberlin that he saw the largest bear track at the big Mound on Lake George that he ever saw, and was afraid to tackle him. Dr. Hamberlin said, "I never saw one that I was afraid to tackle. " Dr. Hamberlin landed his skiff at the Mound and his dogs soon bayed the bear. Dr. Hamberline fired and the ball glanced on the bear's head. The bear caught him by the right thigh and tore all the flesh off. He drew his knife and the bear crushed his right arm. He cheered the dogs and they pulled the bear off. The bear whipped the dogs and attacked him the third time, biting him in the hollow back of his neck. Mr. Wilson came up and shot the bear dead on Dr. Hamberlin. The party returned to Satartia, but Dr. Hamberlin told them to put the bear in the skiff, that he would not leave without his antagonist. The bear weighed six hundred and forty pounds.'

"Dr. Hamberlin lived three days. I knew all the parties. His son John and myself hunted with them in 1843 and 1844, when we were too small to carry a gun."

A large bear is not afraid of dogs, and an old he, or a she with cubs, is always on the lookout for a chance to kill any dog that comes near. While lean and in good running condition it is not an easy matter to bring a bear to bay; but as they grow fat they become less able to run, and the young ones, and even occasionally a full-grown she, will then readily tree. If a man is not nearby, a tired big bear will treat the pack with whimsical indifference.

The Metcalfs recounted to me how they had once seen a bear, which had been chased quite a time, evidently make up its mind that it needed a rest and could afford to take it without much regard for the hounds. The bear accordingly selected a small opening and lay flat on its back with its nose and all its four legs extended. The dogs surrounded it in frantic excitement, barking and baying, and gradually coming very close. The bear was watching, however, and suddenly sat up with a jerk, frightening the dogs nearly into fits. Half of them turned back-somersaults in their panic, and all promptly gave the bear ample room. The bear lay flat on its back again, and the pack gradually regaining courage once more closed in. At first the bear, which was evidently reluctant to arise, kept them at a distance by now and then thrusting an unexpected paw toward them; and when they became too bold it sat up with a jump and once more put them all to flight.

For several days we hunted perseveringly around this camp on the Tenasa Bayou, but without success. Deer abounded, but we could find no bear; and of the deer we killed only what we actually needed for use in camp. I killed one myself by a good shot, in which, however, I fear that the element of luck played a considerable part. We had started as usual by sunrise, to be gone all day; for we never counted upon returning to camp before sunset. For an hour or two we threaded our way, first along an indistinct trail, and then on an old disused road, the hardy woods horses keeping on a running walk without much regard to the difficulties of the ground. The disused road lay right across a great cane-brake, and while some of the party went around the cane with the dogs, the rest of us strung out along the road so as to get a shot at any bear that might come across it. I was following Harley Metcalf, with John McIlhenny and Doctor Rixey behind on the way to their posts, when we heard in the far-off distance two of the younger hounds, evidently on the trail of a deer. Almost immediately afterward a crash in the bushes at our right hand and behind us made me turn around, and I saw a deer running across the few feet of open space; and as I leaped from my horse it disappeared in the cane. I am a rather deliberate shot, and under any circumstances a rifle is not the best weapon for snap-shooting, while there is no kind of shooting more difficult than on running game in a cane-brake. Luck favored me in this instance, however, for there was a spot a little ahead of where the deer entered in which the cane was thinner, and I kept my rifle on its indistinct, shadowy outline until it reached this spot; it then ran quartering away from me, which made my shot much easier, although I could only catch its general outline through the cane. But the .45-70 which I was using is a powerful gun and shoots right through cane or bushes; and as soon as I pulled the trigger the deer, with a bleat, turned a tremendous somersault and was dead when we reached it. I was not a little pleased that my bullet should have sped so true when I was making my first shot in company with my hard-riding, straight-shooting planter friends.

But no bear were to be found. We waited long hours on likely stands. We rode around the cane-brakes through the swampy jungle, or threaded our way across them on trails cut by the heavy wood knives of my companions; but we found nothing. Until the trails were cut the cane-brakes were impenetrable to a horse and were difficult enough to a man on foot. On going through them it seemed as if we must be in the tropics; the silence, the stillness, the heat, and the obscurity, all combining to give a certain eeriness to the task, as we chopped our winding way slowly through the dense mass of close-growing, feather-fronded stalks. Each of the hunters prided himself on his skill with the horn, which was an essential adjunct of the hunt, used both to summon and control the hounds, and for signaling among the hunters themselves. The tones of many of the horns were full and musical; and it was pleasant to hear them as they wailed to one another, backward and forward, across the great stretches of lonely swamp and forest.

A few days convinced us that it was a waste of time to stay longer where we were. Accordingly, early one morning we hunters started for a new camp fifteen or twenty miles to the southward, on Bear Lake. We took the hounds with us, and each man carried what he chose or could in his saddle-pockets, his slicker on his horse's back behind him. Otherwise we took absolutely nothing in the way of supplies, and the Negroes with the tents and camp equipage were three days before they overtook us. On our way down we were joined by Major Amacker and Doctor Miller, with a small pack of cathounds. These were good deer-dogs and they ran down and killed on the ground a good-sized bobcat - a wildcat, as it is called in the South. It was a male and weighed twenty-three and a half pounds. It had just killed and eaten a large rabbit. The stomachs of the deer we killed, by the way, contained acorns and leaves.

Our new camp was beautifully situated on the bold, steep bank of Bear Lake - a tranquil stretch of water, part of an old river-bed, a couple of hundred yards broad, with a winding length of several miles. Giant cypress grew at the edge of the water, the singular cypress knees rising in every direction round about, while at the bottoms of the trunks themselves were often cavernous hollows opening beneath the surface of the water, some of them serving as dens for alligators. There was a waxing moon, so that the nights were as beautiful as the days.

From our new camp we hunted as steadily as from the old. We saw bear sign, but not much of it, and only one or two fresh tracks. One day the hounds jumped a bear, probably a yearling from the way it ran; for at this season a yearling or two-year-old will run almost like a deer, keeping to the thick cane as long as it can and then bolting across through the bushes of the ordinary swamp-land until it can reach another cane-brake. After a three hours' run this particular animal managed to get clear away without one of the hunters ever seeing it, and it ran until all the dogs were tired out. A day or two afterward one of the other members of the party shot a small yearling; that is, a bear which would have been two years old in the following February. It was very lean, weighing but fifty-five pounds. The finely chewed acorns in its stomach showed that it was already beginning to find mast.

We had seen the tracks of an old she in the neighborhood, and the next morning we started to hunt her out. I went with Clive Metcalf. We had been joined overnight by Mr. Ichabod Osborn and his son Tom, two Louisiana planters, with six or eight hounds - or rather bear-dogs, for in these packs most of the animals are of mixed blood, and, as with all packs that are used in the genuine hunting of the wilderness, pedigree counts for nothing as compared with steadiness, courage, and intelligence. There were only two of the new dogs that were really stanch bear-dogs. The father of Ichabod Osborn had taken up the plantation upon which they were living in 1811, only a few years after Louisiana became part of the United States, and young Osborn was now the third in line from father to son who had steadily hunted bears in this immediate neighborhood.

On reaching the cypress slough near which the tracks of the old she had been seen the day before, Clive Metcalf and I separated from the others and rode off at a lively pace between two of the cane-brakes. After an hour or two's wait we heard, very far off, the notes of one of the loudest-mouthed hounds, and instantly rode toward it, until we could make out the babel of the pack. Some hard galloping brought us opposite the point toward which they were heading - for experienced hunters can often tell the probable line of a bear's flight, and the spots at which it will break cover. But on this occasion the bear shied off from leaving the thick cane and doubled back; and soon the hounds were once more out of hearing, while we galloped desperately around the edge of the cane. The tough woods horses kept their feet like cats as they leaped logs, plunged through bushes, and dodged in and out among the tree-trunks; and we had all we could do to prevent the vines from lifting us out of the saddle, while the thorns tore our hands and faces. Hither and thither we went, now at a trot, now at a run, now stopping to listen for the pack. Occasionally we could hear the hounds, and then off we would go racing through the forest toward the point for which we thought they were heading. Finally, after a couple of hours of this, we came up on one side of a cane-brake on the other side of which we could hear not only the pack but the yelling and cheering of Harley Metcalf and Tom Osborn and one or two of the Negro hunters, all of whom were trying to keep the dogs up to their work in the thick cane. Again we rode ahead, and now in a few minutes were rewarded by hearing the leading dogs come to bay in the thickest of the cover. Having galloped as near to the spot as we could, we threw ourselves off the horses and plunged into the cane, trying to cause as little disturbance as possible, but of course utterly unable to avoid making some noise. Before we were within gunshot, however, we could tell by the sounds that the bear had once again started, making what is called a "walking bay." Clive Metcalf, a finished bearhunter, was speedily able to determine what the bear's probable course would be, and we stole through the cane until we came to a spot near which he thought the quarry would pass. Then we crouched down, I with my rifle at the ready. Nor did we have long to wait. Peering through the thick-growing stalks I suddenly made out the dim outline of the bear coming straight toward us; and noiselessly I cocked and half raised my rifle, waiting for a clearer chance. In a few seconds it came; the bear turned almost broadside to me, and walked forward very stiff-legged, almost as if on tiptoe, now and then looking back at the nearest dogs. These were two - Rowdy, a very deep-voiced hound, in the lead, and Queen, a shrill-tongued brindled bitch, a little behind. Once or twice the bear paused as she looked back at them, evidently hoping that they would come so near that by a sudden race she could catch one of them. But they were too wary.

All of this took but a few moments, and as I saw the bear quite distinctly some yards off, I fired for behind the shoulder. Although I could see her outline, yet the cane was so thick that my sight was on it and not on the bear itself. But I knew my bullet would go true; and, sure enough, at the crack of the rifle the bear stumbled and fell forward, the bullet having passed through both lungs and out at the opposite side. Immediately the dogs came running forward at full speed, and we raced forward likewise lest the pack should receive damage. The bear had but a minute or two to live, yet even in that time more than one valuable hound might lose its life; so when within half a dozen steps of the black, angered beast, I fired again, breaking the spine at the root of the neck; and down went the bear stark dead, slain in the cane-brake in true hunter fashion. One by one the hounds struggled up and fell on their dead quarry, the noise of the worry filling the air. Then we dragged the bear out to the edge of the cane, and my companion wound his horn to summon the other hunters.

This was a big she bear, very lean, and weighing two hundred and two pounds. In her stomach were palmetto-berries, beetles, and a little mutton-cane, but chiefly acorns chewed up in a fine brown mass.

John McIlhenny had killed a she bear about the size of this on his plantation at Avery's Island the previous June. Several bear had been raiding his corn-fields, and one evening he determined to try to waylay them. After dinner he left the ladies of his party on the gallery of his house while he rode down in a hollow and concealed himself on the lower side of the corn-field. Before he had waited ten minutes a she bear and her cub came into the field. Then she rose on her hind legs, tearing down an armful of ears of corn which she seemingly gave to the cub, and then rose for another armful. McIlhenny shot her; tried in vain to catch the cub; and rejoined the party on the veranda, having been absent but one hour.

After the death of my bear I had only a couple of days left. We spent them a long distance from camp, having to cross two bayous before we got to the hunting-grounds. I missed a shot at a deer, seeing little more than the flicker of its white tail through the dense bushes; and the pack caught and killed a very lean two-year-old bear weighing eighty pounds. Near a beautiful pond called Panther Lake we found a deer-lick, the ground not merely bare, but furrowed into hollows by the tongues of the countless generations of deer that had frequented the place. We also passed a huge mound, the only hillock in the entire district; it was the work of man, for it had been built in the unknown past by those unknown people whom we call mound-builders. On the trip, all told, we killed and brought into camp three bear, six deer, a wildcat, a turkey, a possum, and a dozen squirrels; and we ate everything except the wildcat.

In the evenings we sat around the blazing camp-fires, and, as always on such occasions, each hunter told tales of his adventures and habits of the beasts of the wilderness. One Sunday morning we saw two wolves appear for a moment on the opposite side of the bayou, but they vanished before we could shoot. All of our party had a good deal of experience with wolves. The Metcalfs had had many sheep killed by them, the method of killing being invariably by a single bite which tore open the throat while the wolf ran beside his victim. The wolves also killed young hogs, but were very cautious about meddling with an old sow; while one of the big half-wild boars that ranged free through the woods had no fear of any number of wolves. Their endurance and the extremely difficult nature of the country made it difficult to hunt them, and the hunters all bore them a grudge, because if a hound got lost in a region where wolves were at all plentiful they were almost sure to find and kill him before he got home. In one instance, while the dogs were following a bayou and were but a couple of hundred yards in front of the horsemen, a small party of wolves got in on them and killed two. One of the Osborns, having a valuable hound which was addicted to wandering in the woods, saved him from the wolves by putting a bell on him. The wolves evidently suspected a trap and would never go near the dog. On one occasion another of his hounds got loose with a chain on, and they found him a day or two afterward unharmed, his chain having become entangled in the branches of a bush. One or two wolves had evidently walked around and around the imprisoned dog, but the chain had awakened their suspicions and they had not pounced on him. They had killed a heifer a short time before on Osborn's plantation. It has been my experience that foxhounds as a rule are afraid of attacking a wolf;

but all of my friends assured me that their dogs, if a sufficient number of them were together, would tackle a wolf without hesitation; the packs, however, were always composed, at least half, of dogs which, though part hound, were part shepherd or bull or some other breed. Doctor Miller had hunted in Arkansas with a pack specially trained after the wolf. There were twenty-eight of them all told, and on this hunt they ran down and killed unassisted four full-grown wolves, although some of the hounds were badly cut. None of my companions had ever known of wolves actually molesting men, but Mr. Ichabod Osborn's son-in-law had a queer adventure with wolves while riding alone through the woods one late afternoon. His horse acting nervously, he looked about and saw that five wolves were coming toward him. One was a bitch, the other four were males. They seemed to pay little heed to him, and he shot one of the males, which crawled off. The next minute the bitch ran straight toward him and was almost at his stirrup when he killed her. The other three wolves, instead of running away, jumped to and fro, growling, with their hair bristling, and he killed two of them; whereupon the survivor at last made off. He brought the scalps of the three dead wolves home with him.

Near our first camp was the carcass of a deer, a yearling buck, which had been killed by a cougar. When first found, the wounds on the carcass showed that the deer had been killed by a bite in the neck at the back of the head; but there were scratches on the rump as if the panther had landed on its back. One of the Negro hunters, Brutus Jackson, evidently a trustworthy man, told me that he had twice seen cougars, each time under unexpected conditions.

Once he saw a bobcat race up a tree, and riding toward it saw a panther reared up against the trunk. The panther looked around at him quite calmly, and then retired in leisurely fashion. Jackson went off to get some hounds and when he returned two hours afterward the bobcat was still up the tree, evidently so totally scared that he did not wish to come down. The hounds were unable to follow the cougar. On another occasion he heard a tremendous scuffle and immediately afterward saw a big doe racing along with a small cougar literally riding it. The cougar was biting the neck, but low down near the shoulders; he was hanging on with his front paws, but was tearing away with his hind claws, so that the deer's hair appeared to fill the air. As soon as Jackson appeared the panther left the deer. He shot it, and the doe galloped off, apparently without serious injury.

# 7

# THE LAST STAND OF A WILY JAGUAR

## By Frank C. Hibben

*This is a tale of a hunt that is not for the tame nor the hunter who wants to spend a relaxing day in the field. This is jaguar hunting in the swamps of Mexico. A pack of hounds are released on a hot track, then you race after them through mosquito- infested swamps where your sweat will mix with swamp water until you can't tell the difference. There will be no time to rest because a cornered jaguar will kill your hounds if you show up too late. On this hunt for Old Bravo in Lost Swamp, the hunters did show up too late and a fearless lion dog nearly paid for it with his life.*

T
he growls and the roar of the dog pack were far ahead. I clawed at the mangrove roots around me; it was impossible to crawl under the things, or climb over them. There was the sound of splashing above the barking of the dogs and I knew the hounds were fighting the cat in the water. One hound barked shrilly. That would be Drifter. Drifter's voice was blotted out as though a giant hand had closed on his throat. The jaguar had him. Drifter was our last good hound. If the jaguar killed him ....

We should not have been in that part of the swamp, and we should not have been after that particular jaguar. We knew this old spotted cat, or at least we knew him by reputation and we had heard about the place where he lived. Both the jaguar and the lost swamp were impossible. But we tried it anyway.

Dale Lee, who had located the Agua Bravo swamps a few years ago, is one of the two remaining of the five Lee brothers who have been, during their lives, the outstanding hound and cat men in North America. During their careers they have probably accounted for more lions and more jaguars than even such famous oldsters as Ben Lilly. But of the five, only Clell and Dale remain and only Dale still goes after jaguar.

"It'll kill a man, and it certainly kills hounds," Dale often drawls in his slow manner, "but I kinda like it."

This is to say that when Dale said he had found a jaguar swamp which was crawling with the spotted cats, he knew what he was talking about. The swamp which Dale had located is in the state of Nyarit on the west coast of Mexico. Along this shoreline, south of the city of Mazatlan, the Agua Bravo swamp stretches for 150 miles. Through the middle of this long strip, the Rio Bravo itself, a sluggish tidewater creek, cuts diagonally northwest to the sea.

During the last few years, Dale has taken some dozens of American sportsmen into the area and has caught many jaguars there. Dale hauled some flat-bottomed duck boats into the head of the Bravo where the ground is fairly solid. In a clearing near a side creek he established a base camp. From this base camp, Dale took his parties by boat down the many winding creeks into the heart of the Bravo swamps. It's real hunting, as any mosquito-bitten survivor of these junkets can testify. Dale fits each of his customers with a pair of basketball sneakers and tells them not to try to keep dry. This last advice is really unnecessary--either in the boat or out of it, a jaguar hunter is never dry from the time he starts with Dale to the time he comes back to the base camp.

As it would be almost impossible to stagger through the mangrove-edged creeks looking for a jaguar track, Dale has worked out a system for locating the cats. During the mating season, jaguars roar very much like an African lion. As a matter of fact, both male and female jaguars sometimes roar on any occasion.

Dale had rigged up a large gourd, cut open at one end, and covered with a sheet of rawhide like an Indian drum. Attached to the drum head is a thong rubbed with resin. By pulling the thong between his thumb and forefinger in a jerky motion, Dale can make a grunting roar which sounds more like a jaguar than another jaguar. Dale has been so successful with this "bromadura," or roarer, that on several occasions he has called cats up within a few feet. One time, in the Bravo swamps, when Dale and his brother Clell were hunting in a native dugout canoe, a jaguar answered the call so enthusiastically that the cat swam out and threatened to climb into the canoe with them. They beat him off with a wooden paddle.

By calling jaguars during the night, Dale is able to locate one of the cats so that he can put the hounds on a fresh track at daylight. If a jaguar keeps answering and the client stays with him, it is an almost foolproof system. That is, it is a system for anyone fool enough to want a jaguar that badly. Chasing jaguars in the Bravo swamps is worse on dogs than on men. During all of these hunts, jaguars have accounted for some 20 of Dale's hounds. It is always the best dogs that get killed.

Tom Bolack and I had been hunting with Dale before. We were bitten by mosquitoes and chewed by gnats, and we spend about 10 uncomfortable nights floating around in Dale's boat calling jaguars back in the swamps. We caught one jaguar, too, not far from the base camp, but that in itself wasn't the thrill. The most exciting episode of that hunt was a single night as we floated on the edge of the main Bravo and Dale stroked his bromadura with the "oum, OUM, OUM" of the jaguar call. Over across the water to the west, out of the darkness, a throaty voice answered, "Oum, oum, OUM, OUM!" The hair on the back of my neck prickled as the coughing roar floated down on the night wind. Tom Bolack, who had been sleeping facedown over a boat seat like a bag of wet rice, straightened up. Even Dale stiffened. "That will be Old Bravo himself," Dale whispered. "I'd know that voice anywhere."

Again Dale jerked the thong out of the bromadura. Over across the water, the jaguar answered again. Then there was silence, with the occasional splash of a snook in the water or cry of night bird.

Tom and I were all for trying for Old Bravo the next morning at daylight. But Dale explained to us that his two Mexican guides, Felix and Pascacio, had told him that between the Bravo and the sea were some 10 miles of the worst mangrove thickets in all of Mexico. "Old Bravo has never been out of that place, and we've never been in it, but if you guys want to...."

Tom and I lasted about 30 minutes on the west side of the Bravo. In that time, we penetrated about 100 yards. Pascacio and Felix had understated the situation. Unfortunately, in a patch of mud between two mangrove clumps, we saw a jaguar track. It was twice as big as any mountain lion imprint I had ever seen. Even Dale was impressed. "That'll be Old Bravo," Dale commented. "His feet are as big as his roar."

Tom is not one to give up just because of a few miles of mangrove thickets that no human being can get through. So recently we outfitted another expedition. We told Dale that we would be down a few days before Easter and persuaded a friend of ours, Bill Cutter of Albuquerque, to fly down in his plane.

As we circled low over the swamp in Cutter's plane, Bill was groaning. "Never saw such an awful-looking bunch of nothing in my life," he commented. But Tom and I were jubilant. Below us, between the Bravo and the ocean beach, there were mangrove thickets all right, but there were also several large open flats. These were lagoons, or pools of water, during the wet season. Now, in the spring, they were already beginning to dry. Wide areas of mud appeared with lines of solid mangroves in between. On the mud and in the shallow water there were tens of thousands of ducks, herons, and other water birds that rose in clouds at the sound of the airplane engine. As we clipped the tops of the mangroves with a swinging dive we saw jaguar tracks leading across one mud flat.

Dale met us at Tepic, some 60 miles away, where we could land the plane. Bill Cutter, after one look at our jaguar swamps, decided that he didn't want a jaguar as badly as he had thought. Bolack and I outlined the situation to Dale. From the air we had found a small clearing at the head of one of the side creeks which looked like a good camping place.

It was, if you consider sitting on a wet sponge comfortable. The spot was about 25 miles from Dale's base camp by boat. It took two days to make the trip twice, poling and pulling the boats by hand, to haul in drinking water, extra gasoline, and set up a camp.

On the first night, Dale tried his jaguar call. There was no answer. The second night it was the same. No throaty roar came to us out of the darkness. This was discouraging. Perhaps Old Bravo had left the swamp, or he may have died of old age.

The next morning, with Pascacio and Felix wielding machetes, we began to cut a trail due west from our camp. In four hours of cutting, we progressed about half a mile. Then the dark tangle of mangroves ahead lightened and we broke out into the first open flat. On the mud ahead of us was a line of jaguar tracks. The imprints were big, even for a jaguar. In the mud we could see where the toes were turned out and flattened. "It's Old Fallen Arches himself," Tom said.

Dale nodded. The tracks were fresh. We followed where Old Bravo had crossed the mud flat and had caught a bird roosting in the shallow water. White feathers marked the place where the jaguar had killed and eaten an egret.

We decided not to try for him that first morning until we had cut a trail through the more difficult bands of mangroves between the next mud flats. In that tangle of roots, a jaguar would come to bay and kill every dog we had unless we could arrive on the spot very quickly.

In two days of machete work, Felix Pascacio and Tom Bolack had cut a fairly creditable trail west from our camp through four big mud flats almost to the ocean beach. Tom insisted on doing some of the machete work himself. The only thing that discouraged him was a lamentable occasion when his swinging blade cleaved a termite nest high in the forks of a mangrove tree. With our machete trail through the very heart of the Lost Swamp, we would be able to get at Old Bravo no matter where he went. And through the open flats we could double back in almost any direction.

There were other lesser jaguars, too, judging by the tracks. Dale was worried about his shortage of good dogs. He had lost so many of his best hounds that he only had 11 left and only four of these were top-notch trailers. But Tom and I didn't share his pessimism. We were in a jubilant mood as we tried the jaguar call on the third night.

We had followed our cut trail to the first big open flat in the Lost Swamp. We sat down in the mud. Dale opened the special moisture-proof box in which he kept his bromadura. He balanced it on his knee and gave the long throaty cry of a lovesick jaguar. Far away, out of the darkness, came the answer. Tom and I sat bolt upright. Again Dale called. After five minutes of silence, the jaguar answered. Felix and Pascacio shook their heads. Tom and I knew what they meant. That call was behind us, over in the direction of the Agua Bravo on the other side of camp. All of our machete cutting had been for nothing. But there was no help for it.

With Felix and Pascacio still shaking their heads, we splashed back to camp, got in the boat, and paddled silently across the tidewater creek. In the darkness we picked our way through the mangrove clumps to another open flat perhaps a mile east of camp. Here Dale took out the bromadura and called again. Almost immediately the jaguar answered, "Oum, oum, oum!" The throaty roar was just across the flat. The mangrove leaves behind our backs almost vibrated with the noise.

Dale was whispering with Felix and Pascacio in Spanish. "No bueno-- no bueno," they were saying. Tom and I gripped our rifles tightly. So Old Bravo had moved out of his usual haunts! This was going to be thrilling. Already we could hear the soft splashing of cautious feet in the shallow water.

Dale stroked his jaguar call once again. The answer was terrifyingly close. The jaguar was moving toward us. Roseate spoonbills and roosting egrets darted up from the water as the jaguar trotted closer. The splashing was very near now. In the darkness I could see something darker. I nudged Tom. We both raised our rifles. The dark shadow darted from side to side. It stopped. It ran toward us again, moving jerkily.

Jaguars don't jerk. Another swiftly moving form joined the first, and then another. Tom and I lowered our rifles.

"Como estan, senores?" said a voice out of the darkness. Three dogs ran up to us. Three men followed. One of the men carried a gourd similar to that which Dale still held. "Ah, it is the famous tigrero himself," said the leading man in Spanish as he recognized Dale. "We also have come to try for the old cat who lives in the swamp by the sea."

As we paddled back to camp, Dale said apologetically, "Sorry I taught those natives how to call jaguars." Dale added reflectively, "I offered a reward for news of the old jaguar. But I never dreamed those birds would come way out here in the middle of the night."

We didn't catch Old Bravo at night, and he never answered a call in the seven nights that we tried. We gave the three local enthusiasts a few pesos and persuaded them to pole their dugout canoe the 30 or 40 miles back to their village so that we would have no more competition in the swamp. Two or three lesser jaguars did answer our call, but from different directions and with different voices. We wanted no small fry on this hunt. We were after Old Fallen Arches, as Tom insisted on calling him because of his flat, splayed-out feet.

As Old Bravo wouldn't answer the mating call, we decided to go into the Lost Swamp and track him down. We had cut some additional machete trails between various lagoons so that we could move through the swamp in any direction with fair speed. Our job was made a lot more difficult not only because Old Bravo wouldn't answer, but because Dale insisted on keeping his two best hounds on leash, for if his two remaining reliable trailers got killed, we were finished.

In three days of circling in the Lost Swamp, we had found a lot of places where Old Bravo had been but not the place where he was. There was no doubt that the old jaguar was feeding on birds and turtles.

On our fourth day of hunting, just at daylight, we ran into him. We didn't find him. He found us. Dale had turned old Drifter loose as a strike dog. There seemed little likelihood that we were going to find fresh tracks anyway. Drifter and Old Bravo met nose to nose in the machete trail. We heard the jaguar growl first. Drifter snarled. There was a flurry of sound. Drifter gave the squealing bark of a dog looking at game. Two hounds that Pascacio held darted forward and jerked Pascacio face down in the mud. Dale was already running ahead.

As we rounded the corner in the trail, the jaguar, with Drifter close behind, jumped into the mangroves. We couldn't see them but we could hear them and they were close. Dale quickly unnecked two of the younger dogs.

"This will warm up the chase a bit, but I'll keep these others..."

Dale's words were drowned in a roar of barking and splashing. All the loose dogs had got to the jaguar and were fighting.

The sound of the hounds quickly moved away. The jaguar was running again, running and fighting. The hounds which we still held on short leashes tried to drag us into the mangrove roots. But no man could get through that awful stuff without cutting a trail. Tom and I made a quick decision--he and Dale would go ahead to the next open flat and go down that one to get ahead of the chase. I would go back to the last opening we had crossed and parallel the fight from that side. Either way the chase turned, we'd have him.

As Felix and I ran along the mud we crossed a line of fresh tracks. There was no mistaking those big splayed-out imprints. It was Old Bravo all right. He had walked from there not 10 minutes before when he bumped into Drifter on the trail.

Old Bravo knew his swamp better than we did. He never crossed one of the open flats where dogs and men would have had the advantage but stayed in the mangroves and in the water. A mile from where Drifter had jumped him, he climbed a tree.

Tom and I got to the tree together, both badly winded. The old jaguar was about 15 feet above our heads on a dead mangrove. All of the dogs were below. This was too easy. I took a quick picture. When Tom had quieted his breathing, he raised his .30/30 rifle. Now that we were face to face with Old Bravo, I was almost disappointed. As he turned to snarl at us, I saw that most of his teeth were gone. No wonder he had been eating birds and turtles.

His frame was big, but he was not fat. His paws were enormous where they clutched the dead mangrove which was none too big to support his weight.

"Kill him dead, Tom," Dale whispered. At that instant the mangrove branch broke. Even the jaguar was surprised. The dogs scattered. Old Bravo landed on his feet. Tom still stood there with his .30/30 pointed at the sky.

The big cat was up and away. Before the startled hounds could move, the jaguar had jumped in a long leap into the mangroves and was gone. It was seconds before Dale could drag two of the dogs to the place and shove their noses into the hot scent. None of the hounds had seen him go.

"If we ever get up to him again, don't stand around fooling with that camera," Dale snarled as we started off.

We had only been at the tree a few seconds. Not only that, but it was Tom's jaguar. Both Tom and I were pretty abashed at missing our chance. It might be our only chance.

I directed Tom back the way I had come to the open flat. If he ran along the edge of the mangroves a few hundred yards, he could get ahead of the chase. "When you see him, shoot him," I yelled .

With Felix and two spare dogs on a leash, I doubled back through the mangroves to our machete trail. From there I could hit an open-water lagoon through which I could wade for a mile or so. If Old Bravo turned to the westward again, we'd have him between us. With the two fresh dogs that we dragged along, Old Bravo could not get away.

He didn't either. Felix and I splashed through a screen of mangroves and there he was. The jaguar had doubled back and come to bay in the water. Felix let go of the two hounds. Even necked together, they cut off the jaguar but did not close in. Behind came the other dogs. Another dog, and then another reached the shallow water. Old Bravo was surrounded.

He fought well. No dog dared come too close. If they did, they were dead. The jaguar may have been old and his teeth broken, but he could move like lightning. Water was his home. The hounds were out of their element. Dale had said not to fiddle with the camera but I did anyway. I snapped a picture, and then another. In the finder I saw a hound lunge. It was Pluto. Old Bravo whirled so fast that I couldn't follow the motion.

He caught the hound by the side of the face. I heard Tom and Dale crash through the last fringe of mangroves. Now they were in the water with the fighting dogs and the jaguar. Another dog jumped in front. Dale was yelling to hold the hound back or they'd all be killed. Muddy water, wet dogs and Old Bravo were a swirling mass of paws and claws.

Tom reversed his carbine and struck downward with the stock at the jaguar's head. Bravo's grip broke. A piece of flesh ripped away from the dog's muzzle. If Old Bravo had been a year younger, he'd have killed the hound at the first bite.

Tom fired quickly without sighting. Old Bravo sank beneath the murky water. Blood welled up with the mud. The hounds closed in. It was finished. In another minute, the old male jaguar of Lost Swamp was a sodden carcass being chewed and mouthed by the dogs.

"He's a big-footed old jaguar for the size of his teeth," Dale commented as we examined the beautiful spotted body.

"His teeth may be broken, and he may be old," Tom replied, "but I wouldn't trade him for any other jaguar in all of Mexico. I'm going to have him mounted whole just as we saw him in that water back there."

# 8

# BUFFALO!

### By John Taylor

### Pondoro: Last of the Ivory Hunters,

### Simon & Schuster, 1955

*Just one look at the Cape buffalo, even a photo or painting, and you know he spells doom for anyone in his path. The buffalo may not be the most dangerous animal in Africa, but he's the toughest brawler. If you hunt Mbogo, you better kill him fast...because if you only hurt him, he will try to kill you.*

*John Taylor was a professional hunter in the early part of the 20th Century. For more than 30 years, Taylor hunted the Zambesi, sometimes staying in the African bush for two or three years with no contact with civilization. Here's Taylor's opinion of the buffalo. Apparently, this tank of an animal has not mellowed much over the past 60 years or so. Mbogo is still bad news.*

The African buffalo is the biggest, heaviest, and most massively boned of all buffalo. He's a magnificent fellow. Next to elephant hunting I prefer the hunting of buffalo to that of any other species of big game. I know that except for elephant I've shot many more buffalo than any other animal. But although I deprecate those men who allow the thought of buffalo to scare them, I do not suggest you should become contemptuous of them. Far

71

from it! The African buffalo can hit back and hit hard. What I do say is, don't let all the tales you hear about the African buffalo start your imagination working overtime, so that you get all steamed up and are scared stiff before you ever see your first buffalo. I've met a number of men who have done just that. They were so frightened that they completely lost their heads when they got their chance for a shot. They seemed to have the notion that a buffalo will attack the instant he sees you, even though you haven't fired or in any way interfered with him. There are others who believe that a buffalo will invariably whip around and charge the moment he feels the lead if you don't kill him stone-dead with your first shot. I'm not making any dogmatic statements, but I have never experienced such a charge in all the years I've been hunting buffalo --and I've killed close to twelve hundred of them. It's possible that you might experience such a charge; I can only say that I never have, and give it as my belief, based on personal experience, that such an instantaneous charge would be definitely exceptional--unique. I am, of course, referring to an unwounded buffalo. The situation is entirely different if you are following up or have encountered a buff that has been recently wounded either by yourself or someone else. But then, we all know that wounded buff can be horribly dangerous. He's quite a different proposition.

The buffalo gained his reputation for savage vitality and fiendish vindictiveness in the days of black powder and lead bullets. It is practically impossible to stop a charging buffalo with certainty with anything much smaller than an eight-bore or a very heavily loaded 10-bore. The animals can, of course, be killed with much less powerful weapons--the trouble arises when the hunter only wounds and has to follow up. Time and again a man would fire, drop the charging beast, and, thinking he was dead, lean his rifle up against a convenient tree or even against the "dead" buff while he sits himself down for a rest and a smoke. And the next thing the hunter knows the buff has come to life and is savaging him to death. It has happened on innumerable occasions, the lead bullet coming up against the mighty boss of the horns, where they meet in the center of the forehead, and failing to penetrate. If one hunter has been killed that way, scores have; but although the African buffalo is a magnificent antagonist he would never have won his deadly reputation had those old-timers been armed with modern rifles and bullets. All the same, you must not despise him. Men who permit familiarity with any species of dangerous game to make them contemptuous are themselves deserving of a real hunter's contempt.

I knew a Dutchman* who professed a scorn of buffalo. "Why they're only cows," he would say. "They're easy." Yet a buffalo killed him. There was another, also a Dutchman, who sneered at lion (though he admitted he was afraid of elephant). He caught a lion in the ribs with his Mauser one day and then strolled carelessly into the long grass to finish him off. But he didn't get a chance to fire again: the lion ripped him open. He had in the same way stated that lion were only cats and were easy. There was another, an Englishman, who reckoned it was bunk to class rhino as dangerous game; but a rhino finally impaled him on a 22-inch horn, which gave him several very unpleasant hours before he died. Then there was another Englishman, one of those know-it-alls, who had shot two or three elephant--lone bulls--and gave it out that there was nothing to elephant hunting, that those professionals who spoke and wrote of the dangers of their profession were merely putting it on so that the uninitiated might be persuaded they were braver fellows than they really were. He was killed by an elephant next time he went out. One could go on like this almost indefinitely. As I have said, the hunter who allows himself to become contemptuous or think slightingly of any particular species will inevitably become careless when hunting, and that is likely to have but one result. Don't let the thought of an animal frighten you before you leave camp; but being cautious is different from being either frightened or contemptuous.

An unwounded buffalo is unlikely to attack, but once wounded he can be infernally dangerous in thick cover--and, like any wounded beast, he will make for cover if there's any around. It's a never-ending source of amazement to me how little cover is necessary to conceal entirely some big beast like an elephant or buffalo which has decided to ambush you. The inexperienced man naturally pictures the animal standing behind the thickest clump of bush in sight and so passes over with the most cursory glance, if that, some lighter, smaller bit of cover on the opposite side of the trail. Yet often as not it's there that the animal is waiting. His very bulk is his best camouflage--that, and the fact that he will be standing absolutely motionless. I once looked clean through a tuskless elephant bull when he was ambushing me behind a sapling no thicker than my wrist, scarcely forty paces away and no other cover about. Had he not commenced to swing out his ears, in all probability I should have walked right into him. You can do exactly the same thing with buffalo. And since a wounded buff will usually be found standing within 20 to 30 yards of his

*Throughout the African continent "Dutchman" refers to a South African of Dutch descent. A visitor or settler from Holland is called a Hollander.--John Taylor

spoor, on one or the other side of it, and if he sees you coming and decides to attack will have sufficient cunning to wait until you have actually passed before charging, you will find it disconcerting to have to swing around for a quick shot in an unexpected direction. (Buffalo are well known for this tactic.) Moreover, you are usually accompanied by native followers, and since the charge may be directed toward them there is all the greater possibility of confusion. The men's agility will usually enable them to get clear without much difficulty, but fear of accidentally shooting someone may make it necessary for the hunter to hold his fire until the charging buff is very close. It has even been known for one of the men inadvertently to bump the hunter and knock him off balance just as he was about to fire. It might be asked, "Then why in hell go wandering around with a gang of spare men?" The answer is that when you are hunting dangerous game, and especially when following up a wounded animal, trackers are not only desirable but, in my considered opinion, essential. It's their job to keep their eyes on the spoor and follow it while the hunter's eyes are constantly roving ahead and around for the first glimpse of the quarry. Remember, far more often than not, it will be but a glimpse you'll get before the charge--if that. Eyes that have been glued to the spoor will inevitably become tired far sooner than if they have just been roving ahead at their own level. Moreover, the quick and hasty glance thrown ahead won't always be sufficient, and you may easily overlook the animal that is standing there waiting for you to come a mite closer. Another thing: If you have more than one rifle with you, you will naturally want someone to carry it for you; and since it's the height of folly to load yourself down with water bottles, spare ammunition, and various other odds and ends in addition to handgun and knife, you will also be wanting someone to carry those things. In addition, if you are hunting for camp meat you should have at least one other fellow to act as guide to the butchers later--if you haven't brought the butchers themselves, that is. Naturally, when following a wounded beast you will tell your followers to keep well to the rear, all except your gun bearer and trackers; but if the chase has been a long one, or the bush very thick, the lads will naturally close up both for moral support, if you're following a dangerous beast and so as not to lose you. They may be very much closer than you suppose.

There have been men who boast they go out entirely alone to hunt dangerous game. In my opinion that's nothing to boast about--quite the contrary. I consider it the act of a fool.

I'm thinking right now of a fellow I knew, a South African Dutchman, who went out alone after buffalo one day although his men begged him not to. He wounded a bull with his Mauser and followed him into very dense bush. The buffalo was waiting not ten yards within the fringe of the bush. The hunter, with his eye glued to the animal's tracks, actually passed the buff, as his spoor clearly showed, and failed to see it. The bull then charged from a range of less than 10 paces. It would seem that the charge came from the hunter's right rear, so that he would have had to turn around to face it. He wasn't quick enough, didn't get a chance to fire his rifle at all, and was trampled and savaged to death.

Back in camp his men had heard the shot and then, as hour followed hour with no sign of their boss, began to get worried. Finally they decided they had better go out themselves to see if they could pick up any sign. They went in the direction from which the sound of the shot had come, finally reaching a spot where a herd of buffalo had been. They then scouted around until they found the place where the herd had stampeded, and then where one big bull had left the herd and gone off on his own-- showing that he had probably been wounded. Proof positive came when they found blood and saw that he had made for the thick bush. They very cautiously entered the bush and there for the first time struck the spoor of shod feet on the sandy soil: obviously those of their boss. They found him in a pool of his own blood, with his unfired rifle beside him. The tracks told the whole story. There was no sign of the wounded bull; he must have wandered away into the depths of the forest.

I must admit that I often go out unaccompanied to shoot a buck for camp meat. But the shot is fired well within earshot of the camp and my men know that there will be meat and start out right away toward where they heard my rifle. They know me well enough by now to realize that I don't waste ammo taking chancy shots. Having killed, I just sit down for a smoke until I figure my men are within earshot of my whistle. Then I blow a blast or two on it to give them the exact position. When they arrive I leave them to bring in the meat, and return to camp alone. I thoroughly enjoy these lone hunts because when natives are along inevitably much of the actual hunting is left to them. When you are out alone you have only yourself and your own bushcraft to rely upon.

There are some general rules. When following up wounded and potentially dangerous animals you must on no account hurry. Move slowly and carefully, rifle ready for instant use, eyes searching out every bit and scrap of likely and unlikely cover. Don't bother about the spoor-- that's your tracker's job, and he'll make a very much better job of it if he knows that he can rely upon you to spot any movement ahead. It doesn't have to be a movement of your quarry: the movements of monkeys and birds can sometimes tell you where he is if you are walking with your eyes and ears open; you may spot some other animal, such as a small buck, looking fixedly at one spot. It's more than probable, then, that he's watching the beast you're following.

If you're careful you will usually spot your wounded buffalo in time to get a shot before he comes--that is, unless the grass is very long or the bush very dense. In the more open types of scrub he may spot you coming and clear off himself without giving you a shot. He has halted to ease his wound, just as any other wounded beast will do--stopping doesn't always mean a charge or ambush. In the thicker bush and long grass he may not have deliberately waited for you, it may have just happened that he was unable to see you coming until you were right on him. In such circumstances a charge is almost a certainty.

The answer to all this of course, is: Don't wound. Take care to kill or cripple with your first shot and you have nothing to worry about. Despite all the buffalo I've hunted and shot, I can honestly state that I've very, very seldom been charged. And of those charges practically all were made by buffalo which had been wounded by someone else. Since there is no telling when you also may meet a buff which somebody else has wounded a day or two previously, it obviously behooves you to be carrying your rifle, and a rifle with a decent punch. You may spend the rest of your life wandering around the bushveld without ever bumping into a buff wounded by someone else--but you may also do so the first day you go out. I know many men who have spent a lifetime in the bush without stumbling across a buff wounded like that, yet I have encountered three or four myself. I would certainly have been killed on at least two of the occasions, and at the best badly mauled on the others, if I hadn't been carrying a powerful double rifle at the ready. The attacks were so unexpected and came from such close quarters that I would never have succeeded in getting a magazine rifle into action in time. I'll tell you of just one to make my point clear.

There had been a Dutchman wounding a lot of buffalo in one district. The authorities sent for me to try and kill them off because they had been responsible for a number of deaths, women and children and elderly men who accidentally encountered them when out collecting wild fruit and firewood. Having undertaken the job, I advised the powers to chase that fellow out of the district because he was a menace. They had done this-- he had left the previous year. During the ensuing months I hunted down and slew all wounded buffalo in the district that hadn't been pulled down by the big buffalo-killing lion that follow the herds. I'd done a good job and knew it. There was no other hunter in the area, and I myself hadn't wounded and lost a buffalo for many years. Accordingly, I had no reason under the sun to suspect that there was a wounded buffalo anywhere in the whole district on this day in question. Still, I'm a hunter of considerable experience and it is my pride to live as I consider such should live--that is, I never become careless, never omit reasonable precautions, never act contrary to established practices which my long experience has proved wise and sound. And so, when making my way through a wide patch of long grass to where I knew I'd find a herd of buffalo, I was carrying my powerful double rifle. My gun bearer, who was breaking trail through the grass, carried my second rifle in front of me.

For no discernible reason I suddenly began to feel uneasy. I tapped my gun bearer on the shoulder and signed to him that I would take the lead. I didn't even speak--I knew this feeling so well that I felt in a moment or so, if I advanced, I would run into very real danger. As I have said before, you must never attempt to weigh inner urges like this against your very limited powers of objective reasoning: You must, without hesitation, accept and act upon them. That is what I did. As I always do when I do not expect to be wanting it immediately, I had been carrying my rifle muzzle foremost on my shoulder. I now reversed it so that I could get it into action with the minimum delay if and when it was needed. I advanced through the grass, slowly enough to be always collected and balanced. And I had gone scarcely 10 paces more when there came a rush through the grass close beside me. As the barrels of the rifle came down into my left hand my right thumb shoved forward the safety. It was then time to fire, there was no time to get the butt inside my forearm, pressed against my side. Had I been carrying the rifle wrong way round I would almost certainly have been unable to get it into action sufficiently quickly. I had no reason to suppose there was wounded buff anywhere around, but as it transpired this one had been wounded the previous day, or rather night, by a native armed with an old muzzle-loader. As well as I can recall, I fired that shot from a range of less than three feet.

"Oh, you fool! You triple-distilled bladder-headed fool! Don't you know by this time that a buff does not lift his head to look at you, but only his nose? And you call yourself a hunter!"

That outburst was occasioned by a piece of momentary forgetfulness on my part before I had acquired the experience I now have. I was hunting for meat for my men and encountered a troop of 25 or 30 buffalo. I let drive at the big leading bull, placing a hard-nose bullet immediately under the great boss of his horns where they meet in the center of his head-- always a most tempting shot. He dropped instantly and I presumed I had blown his brains out of the back of his head I turned my back on him to see if I couldn't get a shot as the animals stampeded in a semicircle past me, and was about to fire when there was a yell from one of my followers.

I swung around, saw my bull on his feet, shaking his head to clear it, and dropped him again with a bullet in the neck just as he started a rush.

This brings up a point you would do well to remember if you ever try your hand at African buffalo. All buffalo carry their heads low, and when they want to look at you they don't lift their heads like other animals (except hogs); they only lift their noses. This means that the face is practically horizontal, and if you try to slip your bullet in under the boss of the horns, which is so tempting, your bullet may pass over the brain and out the back of the head. It will knock the bull out but won't necessarily kill him. You should take an imaginary line between his eyes and place your bullet just below it. Then when you examine your kill you will find that your bullet has actually entered the upper part of the nose and not the forehead.

Let me tell you now about the hunting down of the Maiembi man-killer. He was the last of the wounded buffalo left around by that Dutchman. I have always thought that the hunting down of this beast was one of the most difficult and dangerous jobs I have ever undertaken. The brute had taken up his residence in an impossible patch of impenetrable bush that extended over many acres. He only came out at night to water and feed close around the outskirts of the bush. There were four other big old bulls that lived in there and they had without doubt been wounded in previous years by other near-hunters; but they had long recovered from their wounds, their tempers had cooled off, and they were now quite innocuous. They lived together in a bachelor party--the brute I wanted was still solitary. It is true that if he were now left alone he might become as harmless as the other four, because nobody ever attempted to enter this patch of bush (he'd done all his killing before taking up residence in here); but since the bush abutted on lands near the kraal I didn't consider it fair to the villagers to take a chance on his good behavior. If any of them were late down at the river, which ran along the far side of their fields, they might easily bump into the killer on their way back up. The bull's spoor showed that he came out nightly, crossed the field, and made his way down to the water. He then fed along the river's edge where there was young grass, returning later to the bush for the day.

I mooched around the edge of the bush looking for an opening, but there was none. The greater part of the growth which comprised the patch was fairly free of leaf for about two or two and half feet from the ground but from there up it closed like a curtain behind anything entering. The big buffalo could brush through this, but no man could. And although the greater part of the growth was free of leaf for some distance from the ground, there was other vegetation growing among it which carried leaf and small twigs right down to the ground. Crawling in there to try to hunt any unwounded buffalo would have been difficult but not particularly dangerous, provided you took the greatest care to kill outright. To go in after a wounded man-killer could only be considered as a last alternative if all else failed.

It seemed that my best bet was to try for him by night when he came out. Had there been a moon all might have been well; but just then there was no moon. I clamped a flashlight on the barrels of my rifle. Unfortunately, the cells were nearly worn out, so I sent runners off to try to get me some fresh ones. In the meantime I determined to see what I could do with what I had--and bitterly regretted it afterward.

I went out about an hour after dark, knowing that buffalo must have their water and in a hot district like this would come out of the bush as soon as they felt it safe to do so. I strolled slowly along toward the river, swinging the beam of my flashlight around in all directions. For a considerable time I saw nothing and was drifting slowly back toward camp with the intention of waiting awhile and then trying again (so as to save my batteries as much as possible) when I picked up a very large eye in the ray of light thrown by my torch. I halted and stared at it. It was unlike anything I'd ever seen. As an eye it looked like a buffalo's, but it was only about five inches off the ground. Moreover, when it moved it did so with a curious undulating gait: like a rabbit feeding, and hopping along a bit farther to halt and nibble again. I decided it must be a rabbit, though it had the biggest eye I'd ever seen in a rabbit. Still, what else could it be?

I watched it steadily. The light wasn't strong enough to show up the animal's body even though that was only about 20 yards away; it showed just the eye. And then another eye appeared, rather more than a foot from the first one but one the same level. That must be another rabbit. If the two eyes had been a decent height above the ground I would now have said that it was a buffalo looking straight toward me, but who ever heard of a buffalo with his head so low that his eyes were only five inches off the ground. One eye disappeared and the other continued to move along now, parallel with my own route, but with that strange undulating movement. I strolled along more or less level with it but it gradually got ahead of me. That didn't matter. It was a buffalo I wanted, not a rabbit.

And then suddenly and most unexpectedly the eye soared up until it was about four feet from the ground and immediately in front of me. It was now about 25 yards away and just on the edge of the bush. For the first time I realized it was my buffalo. The brute had been coming back from the river along an old hippo path which had been worn some three and half feet deep there. It was this that had caused the eye to seem only a few inches above the ground, and the roughness of the track accounted for the undulating movement that had deceived me into thinking it a rabbit. It was only now, when the bull scrambled out of the hippo track, that my weak batteries dimly showed up horns and body. I took a despairing shot as the buffalo disappeared into the bush. I heard the thump of the bullet but knew I'd hit him too far back because his head and shoulders were already concealed in the bush. I don't normally shoot unless I'm sure of killing or crippling. But this wasn't a harmless unwounded beast; it was a man-killer which had already been wounded by someone else. As I looked at it, wounding him again could not make him any more vindictive than he had already shown himself to be, while my heavy soft-nose bullet, even though badly placed, would certainly not improve his health or strength. This is perfectly legitimate practice in the case of a man-killer, though naturally I wouldn't resort to it if I could avoid it. However, what I failed to realize was that my firing like that would inevitably put him on the alert in the future. He had never previously been shot at by night, and up to now hadn't associated the bright light of the flashlight with danger. I could have walked right up to him had I only realized in time that it was my quarry I was watching. In the future things would be different. It wouldn't be possible to stroll around and expect to get an easy shot. The instant the bull saw the beam of the flashlight he would make a beeline for safety--or would charge. Moreover, an additional reason, if it were needed, for him to associate danger with light was the fact that he must have got a whiff of my wind just before he received my bullet: That was probably why he had climbed out of the hippo track and made for the bush.

A careful examination of his spoor next morning showed that he habitually left his sanctuary at the same place, crossed the field, made his way down to the water, which was low at this season, and then after feeding for a while made use of the deep hippo track to set back to the bush. Standing in the field about 15 yards from the buffalo's tracks and about the same distance from the fringe of the bush there was a good-sized tree which the owner of the field hadn't bothered to fell. I decided to squat at the foot of this, on the river side, and hope for a shot when the bull came out that night. Accordingly, just before dark I took up my position. I had been sitting there only a short half hour when my quarry appeared. But it was a pitch-dark night and against the black background of the dense bush I was unable to see him until he was broadside-on to me and silhouetted faintly against the horizon.

Unfortunately my flashlight had not been designed for sitting up like this or it would have had a switch which could have been turned on with the rifle and held ready for instant use. My light had only the ordinary side, which meant that after switching it on I had to return my left hand to the forearm of the heavy rifle in order to raise it to my shoulder. And that took too long in the circumstances. I had hoped the bull would stand for just a moment gazing at the light--that short moment would have been sufficient--but he now knew well just what the light portended. He didn't give me a chance. The instant the light sprang out he whipped around and was all out for his sanctuary. My dim light was not enough to show me his outline for a shot before he was gone.

I got up in disgust and returned to camp.

The following night I tried sitting in the same place without a light-- my batteries were practically finished anyway--but except for a visit from a lion which, I think, got an even greater shock than I did when he came around my tree from the opposite side and found me within a few feet of him, nothing happened.

My runners returned a day or so later to tell me there were no flashlight batteries to be had. So that was that.

Well then, there seemed to be no alternative but to try to make my way into that impossible patch of bush by day. Having wounded the bull myself now, I felt it incumbent upon me to kill him. I didn't fancy the notion of that bush, but there was nothing else to be done. I wasn't a wealthy sportsman who could stick around indefinitely: I wasn't being paid for this work (if I had been I would probably have waited until there was a moon and tried ambushing the bull). As it was, I had to kill the brute as soon as possible so as to be free to push along to where I could make my modest living.

Accordingly, the morning after my runners had returned I went out to reconnoiter again. I decided to wait until close to midday as I guessed the bull would be lying down then--and he must be lying down or it would be impossible for me to kill him. I decided it would be best to enter the bush where he was in the habit of coming out. There was probably some tiny clearing around the foot of a tree or under some bush which would give him shade during the hot hours. It would be my job to snake up along his spoor and hope to spot him before he spotted me. The one and only advantage I would have would be that he wouldn't expect to be hunted in there and so might not be on the alert. But it would call for very careful stalking, because if he became the least bit suspicious he would instantly scramble to his feet and then I would be helpless. The bush would completely cover all his vitals and I would see nothing but his feet and lower legs. If he sighted or winded me coming and decided to charge he could trample me underfoot without the slightest difficulty and I wouldn't be able to do anything. My only hope was to take him unaware when he was lying down so that I could see him under the bush. It wasn't a pleasant prospect to dwell on. It was best to think of something else until the time came to get on with it. So I returned to camp and picked up a miniature rifle with which to stalk spur-winged geese down by the lake shore.

By 11 o'clock I was back again with as many geese as my men and I could eat. I drank the pot of tea my cook had waiting for me. Then, taking my heavy rifle, I commenced what I still consider--as I say probably the most dangerous stalk of my career. I would much rather have stalked a wounded lion under such conditions than a buffalo, because a lion's vitals would have been vulnerable whether he was standing or not. However, it was no use wishing; thinking about it would only make me more scared than I already was. Oh, I was frightened all right--make no mistake about that! I'd had enough experience to know just how dangerous a proposition it was, and how quixotically foolish I was to attempt it.

I reached the place where the bull habitually emerged from the bush. My men tried to dissuade me from entering, as they already had before. They also realized that their arguments weren't worth the candle. My courageous gun bearer looked hurt when I insisted he remain outside with the others. But, as I explained to him, he would be unable to help me if things went wrong, and if the buffalo chose to come for him when we were both down on our bellies, I wouldn't be able to help him.

I told the men they were on no account to enter the bush. If they heard a shot, or heard the bull bellowing, they were to wait at least an hour before doing anything. If I hadn't returned by then, they could come and look for me--and scrape me off the ground if they could be bothered to (but I said that last sentence to myself).

As I got down to start the crawl I grinned at my men, thinking to cheer them, but nary a grin responded. Instead they gave me that blank dead-pan look that only the African can produce. They knew I wasn't acting with my usual modicum of common sense, and they didn't like it. As I have said before, the African does not applaud those who take needless risks, stupid unnecessary risks; he looks upon it as plain damned foolishness. In which, of course, he's perfectly right. Far from sneering at me for being scared, if I had turned back now at the last moment they would have been greatly relieved. But I was determined to go ahead.

It wasn't possible to proceed even on hands and knees; I had to lie right down and literally snake along by means of elbows and toes. My greatest difficulty, and a serious and most important one, was to make sure that the muzzles of my rifle didn't pick up sand or other dirt. It was easy enough to keep on the spoor because the bull had used the same track a number of times. I would edge forward perhaps two or three times my own length and then pause for a careful reconnaissance in all directions; then on again for another short distance. The ground was a light sandy loam covered with thick compost--the annual grass fires never entered here. There were no stones or pebbles and remarkably few dry twigs or dead sticks to bother about. The result was that I was able to move in absolute silence just so long as I was careful--and I was very careful!

I cannot give you any estimate of the distance I crawled or the time it took me. At first it was ghastly: sheer hard labor mixed with fright. But as I kept going and became more accustomed to the mode of progress and realized how quietly I was getting along, my spirits rose and I found myself tingling with excitement. I came to realize more fully what I had learned long before: that anticipation of possible dangers is always worse than the actual danger itself. I had scared myself beforehand by thinking of all the unpleasant things that might happen; but now that I was actually on the job I found it was becoming the most thrilling I had ever experienced. It was difficult and dangerous, yes--it would be foolish to forget the danger-- but I knew now that when I eventually placed my bullet where it would do the most good I would derive greater satisfaction from that one shot than from any I had ever fired before.

My greatest danger lay in the possibility that the bull was lying downwind of me. However, there was nothing I could do about that, so it was best not to worry about it. At long last I came to a tall tree with a tiny clearing around its base. It was plain to see that it was used by buffalo from time to time, possibly by that party of four to which I've referred. There was nothing there now but droppings. Still, I welcomed the site because it gave me a chance to stand up and have a bit of rest. Moreover, it suggested that there must be other similar places where these bulls lay. I gave myself a full 10 minutes' rest here and a smoke. I could see no harm in the latter, because if my quarry were lying downwind of me and could smell the tobacco, well, he could smell me also and that would have more effect on him than all the smoke in Africa.

Then on again. The god of hunters must have been on my side that day. When I think back over all the impossible places in which I might have encountered the wounded bull, and then remember just where I did find him, I have much cause to be grateful.

I was continuing to advance in exactly the same manner as that in which I'd started. It was, I suppose, some 15 or 20 minutes after leaving that little clearing under the tree that I found I was approaching another similar little clear patch with a tall tree in the center of it. And there was something else there also, something blacker and more solid than bush.

Some of it was concealed by the tree trunk and some of it extended out to the right of the tree. It might have been an anthill, of course, or the trunk of a long-dead tree--but I had a feeling that it was my quarry. I could only see it indistinctly as yet and would have to go several lengths farther forward to be certain; but I had no real doubt as to what it was. And it certainly wasn't the quartet: The clearing was so small that they would have been lying all around the tree, easily discernible.

I snaked forward twice my own length; and again. Then I slowly took hold of my rifle with both hands and slid forward the safety catch.

The bull was lying down asleep with his nose on the ground like an old cow taking her ease in a meadow. His hindquarters were concealed by the tree, but the rest of his body was broadside-on to me with the head turned away. I could have shot him then and there from where I lay, and I sometimes wonder why I didn't. But apart from the fact that I don't like shooting from the prone position if I can possibly avoid it, there was also the fact that if anything went wrong I'd be at a grave disadvantage. I had, of course, expected to be compelled to fire while prone, but it seemed to me now that it was worth making a major effort to get a bit farther forward so I could at least kneel, and possibly stand upright. So I very carefully inched forward until I was clear of the bush and in the tiny clearing along with the bull, I was now within three and a half steps of him (measured later). And still he slept.

I slowly got myself into a kneeling position, one knee down and the other up, raised my rifle and drove a heavy bullet into the bull's shoulder. He rolled over on his side without a murmur or a kick.

Far from allowing familiarity with dangerous game to breed contempt, I find that the greater my experience the greater my respect. I don't mean by this that I'm growing more frightened; quite the contrary. I used to be scared stiff in my early days, whereas nowadays I'm not--provided I have a decent rifle in my hands and equally reliable ammunition for it. What I mean is that the more I see of wild animals and the punishment they can take, the more I realize their potentialities for mischief when wounded and vengeful. My nervousness in days gone by was due to an overactive imagination playing upon inexperience. There are many others who suffer from the same defect. Provided they realize it in time and have the courage to admit it there will probably be no harm done. The trouble is that so few of them will admit they're scared. They don't or won't realize that there is nothing to be ashamed of in being frightened--it's perfectly natural, and there must be something wrong with the man who can honestly say he has never been afraid when first facing death, whether from bullets, bombs, or a wounded elephant, buffalo, or lion.

# 9

# BROWN FURY OF THE MOUNTAINS

## By Ben East

## Outdoor Life, November 1940

*I can't imagine a more terrifying hunting situation than a wounded grizzly. As Ben writes here, the roar alone will run a chill through most men. But when a grizzly has you in his grip, it is then that you will feel death. Many victims of bear maulings survive the physical beating, but the emotional scars haunt these people forever.*

*So why do men hunt an animal that can literally snap your neck in two with a single slap? Ask any bear hunter and he will try to tell you why. If you're a hunter, you will understand. If you do not hunt, you will never understand.*

*The late Ben East was a master storyteller whose talents will be missed forever. His stories, however, will continue to entertain us for generations. Here is a Ben East tale of a grizzly hunt gone sour. It's one of Ben's best.*

The roar of a wounded grizzly bear is nicely designed to try the courage of a man. It's half snarl and half bellow, and it's full of blood and fangs and murderous rage. And when it comes at close range, when the bear rears up beside a windfall 30 feet away and starts for you, and you realize that no force at your command can keep him from reaching you, fangs and claws and blood and all--well, somewhere in the world there may be a more soul-shaking sound, but just offhand it would be pretty difficult to name it.

If you have any doubts that the roar of a bear under those conditions has the power to turn your blood to water, you might take a jaunt out Jasper Park way, in Alberta, and have a chat with Harry Phillips.

Harry, you see, is in what most folks would consider a position of undisputed authority. He not only knows what a wounded grizzly sounds like at the start of his charge. He knows what follows. He knows the feel of teeth and claws, and the smell of a bear's breath when he's been feeding on carrion for a month.

Not that the knowledge in itself is especially novel. Plenty of men have acquired it in the long history of encounters between grizzlies and hunters. But most of them paid with their lives for knowing. And of the ones who didn't, I doubt whether any had a closer call than Harry. He came about as near to glory, at the hands of an infuriated bear, as it's possible to come and live to tell the story.

Phillips was one of a party of six camped on the north fork of the Burland River, in the Athabasca Forest Reserve, two days by pack train beyond the north boundary of Jasper National Park, four days out the town of Jasper.

The hunters were A. W. Buck and Fred Robinson, sportsmen from Saint Louis. Phillips and Herschel Neighbor were guiding, both unarmed. The game regulations of Alberta do not permit licensed guides to carry firearms while handling hunters. A cook and wrangler filled out the party.

The time was late September. Snow came in the night, the first of the year. A wet fall of about eight inches, and the men rolled out of their bags in the morning to find the trees freighted. Buck, with plenty of experience in mountain hunting, called off his plans for the day.

Robinson, less seasoned, was restless. He voted to have a try for sheep. There was likely country about three miles from camp. Snow means good sheep hunting, makes it easy to spot tracks and animals.

Buck was reluctant to have any of the party go out. The horses would have tough going and there'd be danger of a bad fall, no matter how surefooted the animals might be. But his partner was eager for the sheep hunt. Buck didn't want to crimp anybody's fun. He gave in, and Robinson started off, with Harry Phillips guiding.

Halfway to the sheep country the two made a find. They stumbled onto the carcass of a big caribou, apparently killed by hunters earlier in the fall. It was picked all but clean, and the signs showed plainly that a grizzly had done the picking. Most exciting of all, the fresh tracks of the bear led away from the caribou on the new snow.

Robinson was ready to quit sheep hunting then and there. It was grizzly he wanted, and he was all for taking the track, but Harry talked him out of it. "That bear's probably ten miles away from here by now," the guide explained.

But the bighorn range yielded nothing, and in the early afternoon the two men rode back to the caribou bones. Robinson still wanted to try for the bear, and Harry gave in. "The tracks are going toward camp," he agreed. "We'll follow him for a while, anyway."

They tied the horses and took the grizzly's trail afoot. The hunt was surprisingly short. They had traveled no more than a quarter hour when a big, yellow-brown bear reared up in the brush ahead of them.

He sat erect on his haunches, his forepaws hanging down, his great head swinging from side to side as he tested the wind for definite news of the danger that was following him. Robinson smashed a shot at him and the bear went down on all fours and ran.

When the men came up on the track they found the grizzly was dragging a shattered front foot. The hunt began to take on a slightly different tone from the point. Both men knew the price of carelessness, for it's the trick of a wounded grizzly to double back on his track and ambush his pursuers. Phillips knew, too, the added chance he took by carrying no rifle.

They followed the bear around the side of the mountain, and finally Harry called a brief halt.

"We're getting pretty far away from the horses," he explained. "I'll go back and bring 'em up. You can follow the bear, but take it easy and be careful. Remember, a crippled silvertip is bad medicine at close quarters!"

He turned back; and Robinson went on alone, working slowly. For a second time, then, the grizzly showed himself, moving through brush on the mountain ahead.

Robinson placed his shot in the body. It knocked the bear down, sent him sliding and rolling down the slope 50 feet or more. He gathered himself up and was out of sight before Fred could shoot again. From that point on the track showed heavy bleeding. It developed later that the slug from Robinson's .35-caliber rifle had struck high in the hip and ripped into the abdomen of the grizzly, breaking no bones but inflicting a wound from which the animal would have died finally of hemorrhage.

Robinson trailed slowly after that to give Phillips a chance to overtake him. A half mile farther along, he came to the edge of a thick windfall, stopped for a minute, and something in motion along the far edge of the windfall caught his eye.

It was the head of the grizzly.

The bear was walking along the side of the log jam, carrying his head high. Robinson could see the big, broad skull plainly. There was a chance for a head shot. Robinson weighed the odds in his mind. He recalled bear talk he had heard the previous autumn in the Jackson Hole country. A veteran guide had warned that a wounded grizzly is likely to charge if overtaken in an open spot, where he can come downhill, or across clear ground. There's not much chance he'll try it uphill or through tangles.

This was decidedly not open ground. All the same, the bear was uncomfortably close. Robinson decided to wait for a better chance. He backed away from the windfall, picked an open spot, and waited for the guide to return.

Phillips came up within a few minutes. Robinson told him what had happened, said he believed the bear was badly hurt and was trying to locate them by scent. The rest of the hunt, the two men agreed, was going to call for plenty of caution to avert disaster.

They moved carefully around the windfall, picked up the tracks of the grizzly leading away from the other side, called another halt for several minutes while they discussed the situation. When they took up the trail again, it was with both men well on the uphill side of the tracks, Robinson above Phillips. The guide repeated his warning that the bear might watch his back track, lying in wait for them. The atmosphere of the hunt was growing decidedly electric.

"I'll stay down where I can see the tracks--you stay where you can see me," Harry instructed. Within 50 yards they came to a second windfall that blocked their way, and made it necessary for both men to swing down onto the beat trail to go around the jam. They arrived together where the lower tip of the windfall ended in a thick clump of young spruce, growing out of the mountainside at an angle.

Phillips started to go around the thick tangle. Robinson, unwilling to let the unarmed guide take the lead, scrambled up beside him, turned half sidewise to force his way between the branches and Harry. And just ahead of them, not more than 30 feet away, the roar of an enraged bear exploded like a bomb of sound!

Thirty miles an hour is probably a conservative estimate of the speed of a charging grizzly. Forty might not be too high. Pace off 30 feet on your front lawn, imagine 700 pounds of bear covering it at 40 miles an hour, and you'll have the picture.

Robinson shot from his side, with the stock of the rifle still tucked under his arm, with no time to bring it up.

The soft-nosed, copper-jacketed bullet of the .35 rifle weighs 200 grains. It leaves the muzzle at a velocity of 2,180 feet per second. At 20 feet it delivers a jabbing, jolting, paralyzing wallop of better than 2,000 foot-pounds. That's enough to lift a ton more than one foot off the ground.

The grizzly absorbed that blow and never flinched. Robinson didn't even know that his shot had hit the bear.

Later he learned that the slug had struck the bridge of the grizzly's nose two or three inches below the crossline of the eyes, mushroomed according to formula, gone literally down the bear's throat, and expanded the rest of its momentum in the chest. Four inches higher on the target would have dropped the grizzly stone-dead in his tracks.

The bear came on without faltering, snarling and snapping from side to side like a mad dog. He did not rear up, but struck as a bull strikes, charging into the men full tilt. It was Phillips he had seen and was after, but the men were standing a couple of feet apart and he smashed into both of them. His shoulder or the side of his body hit Robinson and sent him sprawling back, clear of the spruce clump. The hunter landed, by no means gently, in a sitting position 10 or a dozen feet away. Through the rest of the fracas he escaped all attention from the bear. It was Phillips the grizzly was determined to finish off.

When Robinson regained his feet, the bear and Harry had slid eight or 10 yards down the side of the mountain. The grizzly was standing over the man, tearing at him, and in the back of Robinson's mind Phillips's one unearthly yell was still ringing.

That one scream was all he heard from Harry. In fact it was all Harry had been capable of, but if Fred Robinson lives to be a very old man he stands little chance of ever forgetting it.

More than one big-game hunter, speculating on the sensations of a man mauled to death by one of the large carnivores, has voiced the belief that a merciful coma sets in at the outset of the attack. That the nerve shock serves as a powerful drug, a sedative that dulls the senses to pain and fear alike, making the death an easy one. Maybe so. Or maybe the breath was knocked out of Harry Phillips when he went down under the impact of the bear's charge. Anyway, all he was able to recall afterwards was hazy thought, to the effect that maybe the bear would leave him for dead if he did not move.

Robinson scrambled to his feet with that one scream loud in his ears, and looked around for his rifle to finish the affair. The rifle was gone.

It had flown out of Fred's hands when the bear knocked him down. In the tangle of fallen timber and rock and spruce, with half a foot of snow on the ground, the chances were all against finding the rifle soon. And unless it was found very soon it wouldn't do any good.

What Robinson did next he didn't talk about for quite some time. He had been home weeks before he finally sketched in this part of the story to Buck, and then it was with the apologetic remark that he didn't expect or want anybody to believe him.

There was Phillips and the grizzly, 20 or 30 feet away down the side of the mountain, with the bear tearing at the man. There was only one thing to do, and Robinson did it by instinct, not by reason. He reached back and unsnapped the leather loop around the handle of his hunting knife. Something in the back of his mind told him that if he ran down and stuck the knife into the bear's side the grizzly would turn his attention from Harry. And he didn't take time to figure what would happen to either of them, after that.

"I didn't do it because of bravery," he told Buck afterward, scoffing at his own solution. "I did it because I had to do something."

He started down for the bear, freeing the knife as he went. But before he had it clear of the sheath the picture changed again.

Running those few paces down the slope toward the bear, Fred saw his rifle. The grizzly was standing on it. On the barrel, with one hind foot. The stock was sticking out from under the foot at a crazy angle.

The rifle looked all right. Fred didn't wait to see whether it had been damaged. He grabbed it and yanked it out from under the bear's foot.

Quarters were pretty close by that time. The bear must have felt the movement under his foot. He dropped the business of finishing Phillips, raised his head, and looked around over his shoulder at the newcomer.

He was a sight Fred Robinson won't be likely to forget for quite some time. He had been mauling Harry about the head, and he had bitten through the guide's felt hat. When he looked around at Fred he was champing his blood-flecked jaws on the hat, trying to rid himself of the thing. It was plain he wanted to clear the decks for further action.

Had Robinson pumped another shell into the chamber of the rifle after that frenzied snapshot as the bear charged? He couldn't remember. Had he replaced in the magazine any of the shells he had used? He didn't remember that, either. Was the gun empty in either the chamber or magazine or both? He didn't know. At the moment he had just one idea. To hold the muzzle of the rifle to the bear's head and snap the trigger.

Robinson guessed afterward that the front sight of his rifle was four feet from the head of the grizzly when he squeezed off the trigger. The estimate is probably a generous one.

The 200-grain slug struck just under the ear, and the bear went down as if hit by a lightning bolt, stone-dead in his tracks.

Harry lay under the bear, silent and inert. Fred rubbed snow on his face and worked over him for a couple of minutes, breathing a sigh of relief when the guide moved, flicked back to half consciousness.

Not that Harry's predicament was ended, by any means. The bear, all 700 pounds, was lying squarely on top of him. The pelt later measured eight feet from tip to tip and eight feet across, which gives you an idea.

Besides, the guide was horribly mauled. The bear had bitten through the thick flesh on the inside of one leg--bitten the full length of his great fangs. He had driven the claws of his sound forefoot deep into the other leg, between knee and hip, tearing loose thick ribbons of flesh that hung down like tattered bloody rags.

Sometime in the fracas Harry must have reached up with his right hand in a desperate effort to fend off the grizzly's attack. For his pains the bear had bitten the index finger neatly off at the second joint, leaving it dangling by a thread of tendon. The guide's head was in the worst shape of all. The grizzly had had Harry's whole head between his jaws. His lower fang went into the forehead just over the right eye, missing the arch of the eye orbit by no more than a quarter of an inch. To that margin Phillips probably owes his life. The smooth, round bone of the skull gave the bear no purchase for his powerful jaws. Meanwhile, his upper fang had cut into the scalp above the forehead on the left side, gone to the bone and inflicted a slash three or four inches long.

Were the grizzly's powerful jaw muscles weakened by the shot that smashed into the bridge of his nose? Is Harry alive because the bear was prevented by wounds from exerting the full might of those great fang-studded jaws? Harry himself and Robinson and Buck say yes. Save for that earlier shot, unlucky as it seemed at the time, Phillips would have died there under the grizzly before Fred found his rifle, they believe.

Robinson went to work to free Harry from under the dead bear. Try as he would he could not roll the bear off or move it enough to free any part of Phillips. Finally he managed to work one foot out. The grizzly was lying squarely on the other leg. Fred braced his feet against the bear's side and tugged at Harry's shoulders. Little by little he pulled the guide free. The second foot came out from beneath the grizzly minus boot and sock.

Harry was still conscious, but he lacked the strength to stand. Fred proceeded to dress his cuts as best he could there on the mountain. First he cut off the finger that dangled by a cord. He hastily disinfected claw and fang wounds, using a small bottle of mercurochrome that Harry carried in his pocket. This checked the worst of the bleeding. Then began the slow, dread trek across the valley to the horses.

Robinson had little hope that they would reach the horses with Harry still alive, that either animal would let him lift the guide into the saddle, reeking as he did of blood and bear, or that Phillips could endure the ride back to camp once he was in the saddle.

But they plodded on, a few yards at a time. When Harry grew sick and faint and wanted to give up, Robinson spurred him by complaints that he could never hope to reach camp without the guide.

They made it to the horses finally. Harry's mount, a wise, patient old cow pony, looked him over, sniffed the bear scent, and stood quiet as if he knew all about what had happened up there on the mountain. Buck commented later that this was one of the most unusual things he had ever known a horse to do. The average saddle animal fears bear smell as much as he fears death.

They rode into camp at dusk, with Phillips half lying across the saddle horn, shaken with cold, all but frozen in his bloody, sweat-drenched clothing, barely able to whisper "Bear!" when Buck asked him what had happened.

They laid him on a blanket in the cook tent, cut his clothes off, put hot rocks at his feet, and went to work in earnest on the bear wounds.

All the cuts but one, that is. When they finished the job of first aid, an hour before midnight, there was one part of the work left undone. That was the severed finger. When Robinson had cut the dangling tendon, there at the scene of the scrap, it had contracted and drawn far back under the skin of the finger stub and hand. With it, it carried inevitable contamination from the carrion-foul teeth of the bear. But it was too deep in the flesh to be opened up and cleaned.

They started Harry out for Jasper early the next morning with Colon, the wrangler. Herschel Neighbor, the second guide, had left before daybreak to push on ahead. At the Jasper Park boundaries lay a ranger's cabin. From there Neighbor could phone into town for a doctor and medical supplies to come out and meet the party.

Herschel made 28 miles to the ranger's cabin by four o'clock that afternoon and put through his call. Colon and Harry did half as well. They made camp in the snow that night. At three-thirty the next afternoon they reached the cabin. A half hour later a doctor rode in.

All in all, Harry Phillips was three nights and four days on the trail, getting down to the hospital at Jasper. And long before the end of the fourth day the contamination left on the torn finger tendon by the teeth of the grizzly was doing its work. Harry was delirious from that infected finger when the little train rode into Jasper.

It was six weeks before Harry saw the outside of the hospital again, and he was still pretty shaky on his feet. But he didn't feel like complaining much. By all the rules he should have checked out, back there on the north fork of the Burland or somewhere on the trail down to Jasper, and he knew it.

# 10

# ROGUE ELEPHANT

## By Capt. Patrick A. Meade

## Outdoor Life, June 1941

*When an elephant turns into a bully, he becomes a rogue. He charges through villages, smashing huts, tearing up crops and stomping any villager in his path. Because of his sheer size and strength, it is not likely that the problem can ever be solved by transplanting or any other method. He must be hunted and destroyed. Because of his behavior patterns, a rogue cannot be hunted in any normal fashion. He must be challenged on his terms. This is the story of such a trumpeting rogue and an unforgettable hunt.*

"**G**agah, jahat!" The cry is rare, much less frequent in Malay jungle villages than that other dreaded warning, "Amok!" But when it does come, women flee from the stinging smoke of their mangrove-wood fires, men drop their spears or fishing nets and--snatching up children too small to run--dash for the flimsy protection of the kampong's strongest hut. Once in the shelter of its few clapboards and many square feet of bamboo, they raise their voices in unison, aided by the frantic pounding on Malay drums and cooking utensils; and if the rogue elephant happens to be in fairly good humor, he will betake his huge bulk and vicious temper to wallow in their rice fields, or trample an acre or two of bananas to pulp.

But the rogue who visited the little kampong on the Straits of Malacca side of Gunong Pulai was not in good humor, and he strewed a dozen huts to the wind, trampling to death four unfortunate old Malays too indifferent or incapacitated to run for their lives.

Elephants are seldom seen in the vicinity of the Gunong Pulai, whose summit is a reservoir, the water supply for a gigantic fortress about 35 miles away at Singapore. Rubber estates surround Pulai on three sides, but the mountain itself is jungle-covered, and the dense tropical growth stretches far to the north. A road leading up the mountain from the southeast--made in haste by contractors' men--is boulder-strewn and rough, but a third of the way up, a little stream spurts from the rocks beneath a huge flame-of-the-forest tree. It makes an exotic picnic spot, and on the day the rogue elephant decided to run amok, I had taken some friends--a beautiful girl and her charming mother--out for a luncheon in the jungle. I also took along my bull terrier, Mike, a 12-gauge (for pigeons or a chance snake), and a sleek, maroon-colored new car.

The day was perfect, and so was the picnic. After luncheon, the mother settled herself with a book while the girl and I went searching for dainty little blue-and-white "pigeon" orchids. We were perhaps 300 yards from the car when Mike growled low in his throat. He was trained to hunt wild boar, and when he turned back toward the car I knew that something must be amiss there. It was, for as Mike dashed back down the trail, the hoarse, squealing trumpet call of a wild elephant echoed through the trees, and an instant later I heard a crash, like cars meeting head on at 60 miles and hour. Unarmed and worried about my companion, and still more so about her mother, I ran toward the sound, the girl behind me. Mike, however, was there a good first, and (with a courage which discounted his size) had tackled the elephant--an elephant which had bumped my car completely off the road.

The brute was stamping around in the jungle, out of sight, and squealing with rage as Mike growled around his legs. The girl's mother was uninjured, and not overly frightened, for the elephant's attack had been very abrupt. The car, however, had its bright newness ruined forever; its spare tire had been wrenched off, both rear fenders smashed, and the rumble seat dented like a battered celluloid ball. Other parts had suffered too, but after giving the elephant time to move away, I got the engine started, and, with much maneuvering, got the car back on the road. Mike returned panting and happy, for hadn't he routed the lord of the jungle? I was trying to make things halfway comfortable for our return to Singapore when a kampong Malay came fleeing down the mountain.

He stopped when he saw us, and too excited and frightened to notice the damaged car, he blurted "Allah be praised! A white man!" (A white man is the panacea for all native ills.) "Tuan, a gagah jahat has ruined my rubber trees and torn down my house!"

I clucked sympathetically and inquired, "Are your children and wife safe, Haji?" He looked bewildered and replied, "Allah know, Tuan!" I was tapping rubber, and seeing that the elephant was truly a rogue, I ran for help. And God is my witness, Tuan, it is truly a rogue that you will shoot."

I told him I knew it was a rogue, and pointed to the car. The old Malay smiled and said calmly, "Now emphatically will Tuan want to shoot the elephant which is not only a rogue, but most surely mad!"

I assured him that nothing would give me greater pleasure, but unfortunately I was weaponless. The Malay pointed to my 12-gauge propped against the battered running board. "But Tuan has a gun, a two-barreled one. Is the Tuan afraid?"

"Not afraid, Haji, but this gun is for birds, its shot are fine like seed." The distressed Malay, however, being a man of the jungle, could only believe that a white man, having a gun and refusing to help, must be frightened.

Suddenly I had an idea which would at least give the now destitute Malay moral support. Once I got the car down from the mountain it would be on a well-traveled road, not more than 15 miles from the city of Johore Bahru. The girl could drive in and telephone the Sultan, a man who'd forgo his chance of heaven for the opportunity to bag a rogue elephant. What is more, she could get the police department to locate my trackers and hunters. Samat and Mahat, in turn, could bring out my rifle and give me a crack at the brute. Perhaps I could even go hunting with the Sultan, and that would be something, for His Highness is a big-game hunter to be envied. However, as it turned out, there was no competition, for His Highness was away.

The two ladies were game, and I left them on the highway, with final directions for my trackers. A hundred yards beyond our picnic spot, no longer pleasant, the old Malay kebun (farmer) turned off of the track into a pathway which led through thick matted jungle, a malodorous spot, with slimy black mud underfoot, mosquitoes which attacked with the enthusiasm of hornets, and leeches that came galloping over twigs to reach bare knees and open neck. But the ordeal was over in a quarter of a mile, and we came out of the jungle into the squatter's struggling two acres of puny rubber trees.

Apparently the maddened elephant had galloped straight down one row, for several trees of a good two-foot circumference looked as if they'd met an army tank. But the hut, once a really substantial affair, might well have been through a hurricane, for not even one of its piles was left upright. The Malay's wife, his four daughters, and ancient mother lamented loudly by the ruins, while his three sons looked on with Malay stoicism.

No one, however, had been injured, and I persuaded the boys, ranging in age from 10 to 16, to accompany me on the elephant's trail. Not that I needed assistance in tracking, for the holes left by the monster's feet were a foot deep, but the boys could relay messages and bring Samat and Mahat up to me by a more direct route. Confident in the ability of my 12-gauge to stop anything, the boys came willingly, and were only too anxious to overtake the gagah jahat so that they could see with their own eyes the avenging fire flash from the Tuan's gun!

The Tuan's anxiety however, was all the other way, and even now, five years later, I can still see every twist in that trail, every strange conformation in the trees, even the changing colors of the jungle, so closely did I watch for huge cocked ears and little pig eyes above wicked curving tusks.

It was two hours after I'd sent off the car that Daud, the eldest Malay boy, told me we were nearing kampong, on the west side of the mountain, which was only a half hour by trail from his father's rubber land. Following the elephant had taken almost an hour and a quarter, so I sent the youngest boy back to meet Samat and Mahat with a message. Ten minutes later, the jungle opened to present a most gorgeous view; in the distance the blue waters of the Straits of Malacca; in the immediate foreground, sweet-scented magnolia and yellow mimosa trees, and some blue-and-white flowing bushes; behind them, coconut and oil palms under cultivation, and near them the dull green leaves and bright yellow fruit of gold bananas. A heavenly, prosperous-looking spot. "There," said Daud. "Behind those meranti trees is the kampong of Mat Slaman."

A moment later we heard the wailing of women, and then saw a ruined village. The maddened elephant had really run amok there, charging back and forth among the huts. A dozen huts had been destroyed, four people dying in them, and three of the ruins were ablaze, threatening the portion of the kampong that had been left standing. As we arrived, the frightened Malays were just beginning to come back from their hideouts in the jungle.

Ignoring the almost overwhelming disaster, Mat Slaman, a graying, dignified man of splendid carriage, came forward with true Malayan courtesy to make me welcome and offer coffee, which, honoring tradition, I accepted. The damage to his huts could be repaired in a few hours, for the materials were at hand in the jungle, but aside from the loss of life--the real loss was to the kampong's most profitable crop, a large grove of cultivated cottonwood trees. There it seemed as though the brute elephant had maliciously tried to ruin the trees which the Malays venerate-- "Do not their pods shelter the souls of virgins?"--trees whose harvest of kapok represented the kampong's one cash crop.

Sulong, Mat Slaman's eldest son, joined us. He was apparently the only person who'd had a good look at the rogue, and he spoke of it with awe. "Wah, Tuan, he is truly a rajah. Old, perhaps seventy years, and his tusks are as thick as my waist, and long--hei!" The rogue had headed as if to circle the mountain, and the Malays agreed that he would probably cross the river and continue northeast toward the plains. That meant 50 miles or more of trailing, but it suited me. I could meet Samat and Mahat, and get into clothing more comfortable than lightweight shirt and shorts. I was still picking repulsive, blood-filled leeches from my body.

I met my trackers, and determinedly took up the trail. The monster, leaving a train of willful destruction, had circled to within eight miles of Johore Bahru. At one place he had smashed back and forth across a Chinese farmer's sweet-potato field; at another, he butted through log pigpens, killing some of the swine and scattering the remainder. We almost came up with him at a point where he had charged a car driven by one of the Danish planters but missed.

Two days, a week, passed and I was ready to give up, for with that solitary exception, he was always a day ahead. Again, however, he doubled eastward, and crossing the railway for the second time he pulled down a telegraph pole and butted a store shed onto the tracks. Then perversely he followed the rails back toward Johore Bahru. We learned later that he had taken a stand in the middle of the track and delayed the Singapore express for 15 minutes. Another 20 miles, and two Malay rattan cutters said they had seen him only two hours before. They had been cutting rattan, when suddenly the elephant appeared in a rage. He had squealed, flung up his trunk, and danced that peculiar little "two-step" which all elephants effect when about to attack. And then, as the Malays ran, he seemed to forget them, and turned quietly back into the jungle. "But, by Allah, he is a giant!"

All that day, tired and exhausted, we struggled through swamp, oozy, black, snake-infested swamp, and to add to our troubles, the rogue chose to follow the highway which cuts the country north to south. And, of course, with Samat, the one-eyed old reprobate, consulting his charms, we elected to turn in the wrong direction.

Then, with all the cussedness of his nature, the gagah jahat got lonesome and came back to look for us! We'd shot a hog deer, and decided (after a good 70 miles of man-killing travel) to rest all day Friday, which is the Malay Sunday. So we ate, washed our clothes, and lazed. Coffee was steaming for our evening meal (delicious coffee for which Mahat had walked 10 miles, and with the aid of $5 persuaded a Chinese bus owner to drive nearly 40 miles more), when suddenly Samat's eyes simply goggled. Turning quickly I saw an elephant standing 50 feet away between two clumps of bamboo. His near-sighted little eyes were plainly visible and his trunk was snuffing in air laden with the strange odor of coffee. We sat petrified, for, with the exception of a towel, I was naked, and my rifle hung on a tree fork, but within reach.

The brute snorted, took a few steps forward, and we dove for the jungle. The rogue saw the movement and squealed that harsh, fighting, nerve-rasping elephant trumpet call. But Mahat saved us, for even as he jumped for cover he snatched a knot of blazing damar gum from the fire and threw it. The knot burst, so he said, into countless flaming embers on the rogue's head. At any rate, the leviathan made off, venting his fright and rage, and we heard the crashing and snapping of limbs for at least five minutes after he had gone.

It was useless to follow, for he wouldn't stop for perhaps an hour, and daylight would be gone by that time. Once recovered from our scare, however, the sight of his wrinkled black hide, scarred with the marks of a hundred battles, gave us encouragement to go on, even if opinions did differ about the state of his tusks. Frankly, I hadn't noticed them, but Samat, who'd been the first to see the brute, claimed that the tusks were long, thick, and in perfect condition. Mahat who had actually stood and faced him, said they were cracked and yellow with age; not worth the trouble of cutting out and carrying back with us.

We had to see the beast first, however--a task I began to think was beyond our power. The next day I was sure of it, for we found that the cunning old bull had slept within two miles of us! He had fed leisurely, cracking down three palms to get the hearts, and finishing with a dessert of papayas and jack fruit. We followed his trail, watchful and wary, and shortly after noon we came up to a stream in which he had immersed himself, and playfully blown water which still dripped from the trees.

Samat, a wise tracker, suggested we take time out to rest before going on to tackle the gagah, which, he believed, was only a few hundred yards ahead. Samat was right, but there was something more than an elephant in front of us, for with startling suddenness, the bad-tempered old rogue trumpeted a challenge, and something bellowed a reply. There was a crashing sound, another enraged squeal from the elephant, more crashing, and a booming, hollow thump. A moaning bellow followed the terrific thump, and we surmised correctly that the rogue elephant had come in contact with another jungle menace, a deadly old bull saladang, vicious with hatred, who had been driven from his herd. So with the safety of my Indian Express .465 off, we crept forward eagerly, but with caution.

The bull saladang was lying, with entrails trampled out, a few feet from a muddy wallow, but to our surprise there was no sign of the elephant. The country ahead was open marshland, only sparsely covered with stunted growth, and we closely examined every inch of it with our eyes. I was just about to speak when Mahat grasped my arm and pointed. Thirty feet away the mud in the wallow billowed, an ear flapped, and the old rogue elephant whistled with contentment as he foundered about.

Some movement of ours alarmed him, and with a grunt and a sucking sound from the mud, he heaved himself up with a surprising speed, looking, as slime slithered down his hide, like some fabulous prehistoric monster rising from another world. Free from the dwarfing influence of the jungle, the elephant was monstrous, but his tusks, grotesquely hung with green swamp weeds, were both broken and cracked by age and battle. We stood motionless, and as the rogue "felt" the air from our alien presence, he faced us almost squarely. Slowly I raised the rifle, and in the fraction of a minute the whole jungle appeared to quiver into silence. My sights came to bear. The rifle exploded, the light breeze carried back cordite fumes, and the recoil jarred me to the toes.

The elephant teetered, but his trunk went up over his head, and a blast of fury shook the air. Why doesn't he go down? Samat shouts, and the elephant thunders toward him. Quick, a heart shot--it may stop him. He's almost on Samat! Thank God the bullet in the left barrel is soft-nosed--the first was hard.

Now the rifle booms again--the elephant goes down plowing the ground. He falls flat, one leg kicking absurdly.

Eight days of trailing around a 40-mile circle, 80 miles through swamp, jungle, and plantation under tropical heat and chilling, tropical rain torrents. Eight days of merciless thorn, and at least one narrow escape from the fangs of a king cobra, and all for two shots at a barn door! Now, looking down on the great majestic form, I forgot the rogue's depredations, and thought only of the pity of having to destroy him.

Samat began to cut portions of the elephant to sell to Chinese "doctors." Mahat unslung the camera. "Take photo, Tuan?"

Hell no! I wanted a drink and a bath!

# 11

# THE CHABUNKWA MAN-EATER

By Peter Hathaway Capstick

"Death in the Long Grass,"

St. Martin's Press, New York, 1977

*When a lion discovers that a man is easier to catch than an antelope, he sometimes turns into a man-eater. When that happens, he will terrorize villages regularly to satisfy his taste for human flesh. Such a man-eater will continue to kill people until he is hunted down and killed.*

*This is the story of the Chabunkwa lion, a man-eater that killed 10 villagers before being stopped. Hunting a man-eater is different. Here is an animal that has lost its fear of man. In fact, it views man as a blue-plate special. And when a man-eater is reported, it must be destroyed. The hunter has no other choice.*

The safari season was over and I was puttering around camp, taking care of the last-minute details of tagging trophies and sorting and packing equipment when I heard from the district commissioner of the area, who had sent a runner with a note wedged in a cleft stick asking me to come on my Single-Side Band radio as soon as I got it. When I had the aerial rigged after breakfast, he answered my call immediately. We went through the usual amenities, the

101

thin-red-line-of-empiah voice hollow over the speaker. I asked him what was up.

"Sorry to bugger your holiday," he told me, "but something's come up. . . . I thought you might be able to help me out. That bloody Chabunkwa lion chopped another Senga last night. The Tribal Council is screaming for action. Suppose you might spare a day or so to pop over there and sort him out? Over."

"Stand by, please," I answered. We both knew that man-eating lions didn't usually get sorted out in a day or so. I lit a cigarette from the flat thirty-pack of Matinees. Well, I reasoned, I'm stuck. He must have already cleared it through my company or he wouldn't have known I was free. Also, one just doesn't turn down official requests from district commissioners, not if one wants to hang on to one's professional hunter's license. I reached for a pencil and pad.

"Right, Cyril," I answered. "What are the details? Over."

"Bugger hit the village just this side of the Munyamadzi--know it?--around midnight last night, so far as the report goes. Grabbed a young man sleeping off a beer bust with two others, but neither of his pals awoke. Smells like that same chap who ate the other bunch over at Chabunkwa, about five miles from this village. We don't have any Game Department people in the area and it'll be a few days before we can get somebody up from Valley Command or Nsefu. Can you give it a try before the trail cools? Over."

"Roger, Cyril, Roger. I'll leave in an hour. Shall I give you a radio sched at eight tonight to see if anything's new? Over."

He reckoned that would be a fine idea. We went through the usual jolly-goods and signed off. I whistled up Silent and told him to get cracking with the normal katundu for a three-day trip. Less than an hour later we were boiling through the growing heat and billowing dust to the village of Kampisi.

Kampisi looked like most villages in Zambia's Eastern Province--shabby and dusty with a ragtag collection of snarling curs and tired-looking people, hordes of spindle-legged children who wouldn't reach puberty. We were greeted by the headman, a born politician who always wore eyeglasses and carried a fistful of ball-point pens despite the fact he could see perfectly well without glasses and couldn't write a letter. Status symbols are as important in the African miombo as they are on Park Avenue. He treated all within earshot to a tirade on the lack of government protection from the horrors of the bush. I asked him why in hell the three men had slept outside when there was a known man-eater in the vicinity.

"The young men thought it was too hot to sleep inside their kaia, Bwana," he replied. "Also," he said, shuffling the dirt with a big toe, "they were a little bit drunk." He shrugged with typical African fatalism. Most Africans believe it can never happen to them, something like the attitude of front-line troops. The millet and sorghum beer the tribes brew and drink keeps fermenting in their stomachs until the celebrants pass into a comatose sleep wherever they happen to lie down. In this case the price of the binge wasn't a headache, but death.

The headman pointed to the north when I asked him in Fanagalo where the lion had carried his kill. Silent whistled for me, and I walked over to see the pool of dried blood on the crusted blanket where the man had received his fatal bite. He had backtracked the lion's stalk, showing where he had lain watching the village, how he had stalked the sleepers, and where he had begun to drag the body. I loaded my .470 Evans double-express rifle with soft-points and stuck another clump of the big cartridges into various pockets of my bush clothes where they wouldn't rattle against each other. Silent started off on the now cold trail carrying the water bag, a pouch of biltong (wind-and-shade-dried meat), and his long spear.

The afternoon sun seared our shoulders as we followed the spoor into the bush and finally found the spot in the conbretum where the lion had settled down for his meal. The prints of the hyena were over those of the cat, and the most we could recover was a tooth-scarred chunk of lower jawbone and some splinters of unidentifiable bone. Silent wrapped the pitiful fragments in ntambo bark fiber and we started back to the village. Too late. There was no point in continuing to follow the cold trail since darkness was only an hour off and we both knew the most heavily armed man is no match for a lion's stealth at night.

Arriving back at Kampisi about dark, I had two hours to kill before my radio schedule with the D.C. I fished out my flask of Scotch and poured a hair-raising shot into the little, scratched plastic cup while Silent recruited men to cut thorn for a boma, or as it is called in East Africa, a zariba, a spiky barrier or fence to keep out nocturnal unpleasantries. I felt the first lukewarm slug burn the dust from between my teeth and form a small, liquid bonfire in the pit of my stomach. It was that sun-downer or three that made you forget the saber-toothed tsetse flies and the pain in the small of your back, like a hot, knotted cable from too many miles bent over tracking. Four wrist-thick sticks of the biltong washed down with a cool Castle Pilsner from the condensation bag on the Land Rover's bonnet completed my dinner. I sent one of the tribesmen to fetch the headman, who came over to my fire. In a few curt sentences I gave him the succinct impression that anything found wandering round tonight would be shot as the man-eater, so he'd better keep his boys on the straight and narrow. He looked hard at the two asparagus-sized cartridges in my hand and decided that would be a fair idea.

The commissioner came on the radio right on schedule to report everything quiet, so far, from the other villages. "Keep on it, Old Boy," he told me.

I did not think the man-eater would kill again tonight because of the size of his meal the night before. Still, I knew that there had been cases of lions killing as frequently as twice the same night and that, anyway, man-eaters have an uncanny way of showing up where least expected. To be on the safe side, I would sleep in the open car with the big rifle against my leg. Not overly comfortable, to be sure, but those two barrels contained better than 10,000 foot-pounds of wallop, which gives a man considerable peace of mind. I'm not the squeamish sort, but when you have just finished putting what is left of a man in a coffee tin for burial, it does give pause for thought. I had hunted man-eating cats twice before this experience: the Okavango man-eater, a famous killer-leopard, and a lioness who had developed a sweet tooth for Ethiopians. I had come close enough, theoretically, to being a statistic on both occasions to never again underestimate a man-eating feline.

I rigged the mosquito netting and took my weekly malaria pill as Silent maneuvered the extra thorn bushes across the barrier. The humidity hung about like a barber's towel, and sweat poured from my body. After fifteen minutes of tossing, I took another bite at the flask and dozed off shortly after.

You don't have to live in the African bush surrounded by dangerous or potentially dangerous game very long before you develop a sixth sense that may mean the difference between life and the alternative. After enough experience, you find, your brain never goes completely to sleep, but, like an army posting sentries, keeps partially awake while the main body sleeps. A parallel may be found in the case of the new mother who awakes instantly at her infant's faintest cry. This reflex seems better developed in humans than in most big game, who have few if any natural enemies. I have walked up to within a few feet of sleeping lions, elephants, and rhinos, who never noticed me. But then, what do they have to fear?

I don't know what awakened me a few hours later--perhaps a sound I didn't remember hearing, but more likely that sixth sense of apprehension. I sneaked my eyes open but saw nothing in the pale moonlight filtering through the tall acacias. I lay listening for long minutes but decided it must be only nerves. Just as my eyes closed, the night was slashed by a shriek that would curdle Bearnaise sauce. Three more unearthly screams followed. I grabbed the rifle and electric torch, pulled the thorn fence away, and dashed barefoot toward the screams. The beam showed nothing as I pounded through the village until I came to a hut at the far side with the door hanging from a single leather hinge. A gibberish man was inside, his bloodshot eyes wide as poached eggs with terror.

I flashed the light around the interior of the kaia. No blood. The walls seemed intact, as was the roof. The soft snapping of Silent's fingers attracted my attention back outside the hut. In the beam of the light was clear evidence of a scuffle, the smooth earth torn by striations of long claw marks. Bending down, I defined the clear pugmark of a big, male lion. I went back into the hut. The man was still staring in horror, mumbling gibberish. Silent entered with my flask, and we were able to get a gagging shot down his throat. Finally, he calmed down enough to tell us what had happened.

He had awakened when his wife stirred to a call of nature. He told her not to go outside, but she insisted. Anatomically unequipped, as was he, to perform the function through the door, she had stepped out into the night, and the lion had immediately nailed her. The man, named Teapot, heard the struggle and the first scream and bounded off his mat to the door. His wife had reached it and was gripping a crossbar that formed a frame for the lashed-on tshani grass. He recoiled in terror as he saw the lion pulling her by the leg until she was suspended off the ground between his mouth and door frame. Suddenly, the upper hinge had broken, and the woman lost her hold. The lion immediately swarmed over her upper body and, with a crush of fangs, dragged her quickly off.

I looked at my wristwatch. The scratched, old Rolex said two hours until dawn, perhaps just about right to permit the lion to feed and get careless. We might be able to stalk him while he was actually eating his kill or intercept him on his way to water before he went to lie up for the hot hours.

"Chabwino, Bwana," commented Silent "It is good. I think we will find this eater of people this day." I couldn't share his enthusiasm. Rooting man-eating lions out of thick cover is not my idea of good fun. Still, we had our best shot at him yet.

We took up the trail at half-past five as the false dawn began to turn the trees into gnarled monsters. I felt that just as the day before, the lion would travel a few miles, then stop to feed, although after the meal he had taken the previous day, he couldn't have been terribly hungry. Silent ruled out the possibility of this being another lion; one glance at a set of week-old prints and my gun bearer could tell you that lion's favorite color as well as his probable political leanings. The tracks showed definitely that we were on the trail of the right lion.

The spoor led through thinning, winter-dry bush studded with thorn, scrub mopane, and towering anthills for a couple of miles, then turned off to the dense riverine vegetation that bordered the shallow Munyamadzi for about 500 yards of depth along each bank. I had tried hunting lion in this cover before, harrying them through the jungles of waxy, green conbretum, a dense, house-high shrub that grows like a beach umbrella with the handle cut off, in hope of getting my clients a quick shot as the cats crossed the open channels between the heavier clumps. It was hard, dangerous hunting that I had quit rather than risk a client's being chewed up. Half the time was spent on hands and knees peering under the dense growth for a patch of tawny hide, hoping, when you saw it that it wasn't attached to a growing halo of teeth hurtling at you in a close-quarter charge. Everything was in the lion's favor in this growth, and I hadn't kidded myself that the man-eater had left it. After all, he had already proven 10 times that he had no natural fear of man-- the fear that can give the hunter an edge.

I thought about Paul Nielssen's mauling in the past year within this same strip of bush, about five miles upriver. A Spanish client, Armando Bassi of Barcelona, a fine hunter, had wounded a good-maned lion, but it had escaped into the thick conbretum before Paul could get in a finishing shot. As the professional, Paul was obliged to earn his $25 per day salary by following the lion and killing it. Nielssen put Bassi up a tree, as is standard practice, and went in alone after it with his double rifle, a .458 Winchester converted from a .450. The lion lay under a bush, after doubling back on his track in a short loop, and watched Paul track past. Nielssen later told me he heard a slight sound behind him, but as he spun to fire, the lion was on him and knocked him flat.

The infuriated cat grabbed Paul by the shoulder and sank his fangs through meat and bone, while shaking the puny human like a jackal with a mouse. For some reason the lion then turned on Paul's legs and began chewing, as I recall, on his left thigh. Armando Bassi, hearing the mauling, jumped out of his tree and ran blindly after Paul. Coming up, he shouted and yelled at the lion to draw its attention and blew the cat's head into pudding with his own .458. Lord, give us more clients like Armando Bassi! Paul owed the man his life and escaped crippling injury, although he suffered a broken femur and a collection of stitches that would have done a Bond Street tailor proud. An animal that can and does kill Cape buffalo with a single bite doesn't waste much time sorting out a mere human.

As we approached the thick cover, Silent and I stopped to peel off our bush jackets lest they scrape against a branch or thorn giving away our presence or position. We left them behind with the water bag after I removed the cartridges from mine. Entering the green tangle, Silent moved just ahead of me in a low crouch, his eyes on the spoor and his spear held in front of his body like a lance. It is normal between a hunter and his gun bearer/tracker that the first spoors while the other covers the possibility of an ambush charge. It's impossible to hunt and track at the same time. The safety was off the .470 and the night sight, an oversized bead of warthog ivory, which doesn't yellow like elephant ivory, was flipped up for fast sighting in the deep shade. We drifted slowly through the bush listening for the crunch of bone or a low growl as the lion fed in the leafy stillness. The damp, soft soil muffled our stealthy walking on the outsides of our feet, the quietest way to stalk, as we slid through the mottled murk with pounding hearts, ringing ears, and stomachs full of bats.

My mind went over the lion charges I had met before: the quick jerking of the tail tuft, the paralyzing roar, and the low, incredibly fast rush, bringing the white teeth in the center of bristling mane closer in a blur of speed. If we jumped him and he charged us, it would be from such close quarters that there would be time for only one shot, if that. Charging lions have been known to cover a hundred yards in just over three seconds. That's a very long charge, longer than I have ever seen in our thick central African hunting grounds. In tangles like this, a long charge would be 25 to 30 yards, which gives you some idea of the time left to shoot.

Ahead of me, Silent stiffened and solidified into an ebony statue. He held his crouch with his head cocked for almost a minute, watching something off to the left of the spoor. The wild thought raced through my skull that if the lion came now, the rifle would be too slippery to hold, since my palms were sweating so heavily. What the hell was Silent looking at, anyway?

Moving a quarter of an inch at a time, he began to back away from the bush toward me. I could see the tightness of his knuckles on the knobby, thornwood shaft of the spear. After 10 yards of retreat, he pantomimed that a woman's hand was lying just off the trail and that he could smell the lion. The soft breeze brought me the same unmistakable odor of a house cat on a humid day. Tensely I drew in a very deep breath and started forward, my rifle low on my hip. I was wishing I had listened to Mother and become an accountant or a haberdasher as I slipped into a duck walk and inched ahead. I was certain the lion could not miss the thump-crash of my heart as it jammed into the bottom of my throat in a choking lump, my mouth full of copper sulphate. I could almost feel his eyes on me, watching for the opportunity that would bring him flashing onto me.

I lifted my foot to slide it slowly forward and heard a tiny noise just off my right elbow. In a reflex motion, I spun around and slammed the sides of the barrels against the flank of the lion, who was in midair, close enough to shake hands with. His head was already past the muzzles, too close to shoot, looking like a hairy pickle barrel full of teeth. He seemed to hang in the air while my numbed brain screeched SHOOT! As he smashed into me, seemingly in slow motion, the right barrel fired, perhaps from a conscious trigger pull, perhaps from impact, I'll never know. The slug fortunately caught him below the ribs and bulled through his lower guts at a shallow but damaging angle, the muzzle blast scorching his shoulder.

I was flattened, rolling in the dirt, the rifle spinning away. I stiffened against the feel of long fangs that would be along presently, burying themselves in my shoulder or neck, and thought about how nice and quick it would probably be. Writing this, I find it difficult to describe the almost dreamy sense of complacency I felt, almost drugged.

A shout penetrated this haze. It was a hollow, senseless howl that I recognized as Silent. Good, old Silent, trying to draw the lion off me, armed with nothing but a spear. The cat, standing over me, growling horribly, seemed confused, then bounded back to attack Silent. He ran forward, spear leveled. I tried to yell to him but the words wouldn't come.

In a single bound, the great cat cuffed the spear aside and smashed the Awiza to the ground, pinning him with the weight of his 450-pound, steel-sinewed body the way a dog holds a juicy bone. Despite my own shock, I can still close my eyes and see, as if in Super Vistavision, Silent trying to shove his hand into the lion's mouth to buy time for me to recover the rifle and kill him. He was still giving the same, meaningless shout as I shook off my numbness and scrambled to my feet, ripping away branches like a mad man searching for the gun. If only the bloody Zambians would let a hunter carry sidearms! Something gleamed on the dark earth, which I recognized as Silent's spear, the shaft broken halfway. I grabbed it and ran over to the lion from behind, the cat still chewing thoughtfully on Silent's arm. The old man, in shock, appeared to be smiling.

I measured the lion. Holding the blade low with both hands, I thrust it with every ounce of my strength into his neck, feeling the keen blade slice through meat and gristle with surprising ease. I heard and felt the metal hit bone and stop. The cat gave a horrible roar and released Silent as I wrenched the spear free, the long point bright with blood. A pulsing fountain burst from the wound in a tall throbbing geyser as I thrust it back again, working it with all the strength of my arms. As if brain-shot he instantly collapsed as the edge of the blade found and severed the spinal cord, killing him at once. Except for muscular ripples up and down his flanks, he never moved again. The Chabunkwa man-eater was dead.

Ripping off my belt, I placed a tourniquet on Silent's tattered arm. Except for the arm and some claw marks on his chest, he seemed to be unhurt. I took the little plastic bottle of sulfathiozole from my pocket and worked it deeply into his wounds, amazed that the wrist did not seem broken, although the lion's teeth had badly mangled the area. He never made a sound as I tended him, nor did I speak. I transported him in a fireman's carry to the water, where he had a long drink, and then I returned to find the rifle, wedged in a low bush. I went back and once more put the gunbearer across my shoulders and headed for the village.

Silent's injuries far from dampened the celebration of the Sengas, a party of whom went back to collect our shirts and inspect the lion. As I left in the hunting car to take Silent to the small dispensary some 75 miles away, I warned the headman that if anyone so much as disturbed a whisker of the lion for juju, I would personally shoot him. I almost meant it, too. That lion was one trophy that Silent had earned.

The doctor examined Silent's wounds, bound them, and gave him a buttful of penicillin against likely infection from the layers of putrefied meat found under the lion's claws and on his teeth, then released him in my care. We were back at the Senga village in late afternoon, the brave little hunter grinning from the painkiller I had given him from my flask.

I snapped a couple of pictures of the lion with the self-timer and began to skin him. I would later report that the hide had spoiled and was not taken, so I wouldn't have to turn in more than the ears to the Game Department, which claims all unlicensed trophies. Actually, I had it salted and presented it to Silent, who believed that sleeping on it would bring back much of the romance of his youth. When I dropped him off at his village, near my safari camp, his fat, young wives seemed to concur as they bore him off to his hut with much giggling.

The Sengas retrieved the body of the lion's last victim, which was about half eaten. That night, back in my own camp, I took a long bath and sat smoking in the tub, with a tall glass of man's best friend at my elbow. Only now did I realize how close I had come to being the Chabunkwa lion's eleventh victim. My side was starting to turn a lovely black and blue where the lion had hit me, but whether it was from a paw stroke or just the 450 pounds of impact, I didn't know. Academic at best. In this kind of business you learn to remember close calls only for what they taught you, not for how they might have turned out. I took away one lesson for sure: The next time a district commissioner asks me for a favor, I'm going to have a severe attack of radio trouble.

# 12

# GRIZZLY WITH A GRUDGE

## By Dan Ludington as told to James Doherty

## Outdoor Life, November 1959

*If there's one thing more unpredictable than a grizzly, it's a sow grizzly with a cub. To make matters worse, this particular sow may have been nursing an old wound. Whatever the problem, this sow was blaming man and she was going to even the score. Dan Ludington was a foreman for the Alaska Road Commission and it was his misfortune to cross paths with this Alaska grizzly. This is a chilling, true tale with a not so pleasant outcome. Ludington never hunted grizzlies again.*

should have cut and run clear out of Alaska that snowy October morning nearly 10 years ago when Jerry Luebke kicked open the door of my lodge at Summit Lake. Unfortunately, my crystal ball wasn't working. I hadn't seen the big guy in weeks, and anyway I'd always pictured fate as a frowner, which Jerry certainly was not. He was grinning giant in a size 44 wolfskin parka--an old friend with whom I'd shared many a campfire.

Now, 10 years is usually enough time to take the edge off the memory of any run-of-the-mine day. For me, however, this was to be no ordinary day. Jerry's first words--delivered after my two kids, Milton, then four years old, and Rendy, two, had been shooed off his knee--come to me as clearly now as they did a decade ago.

"I hate to tell you this, Dan," he said laconically, "but you and Maxine are about to have visitors. If not today, then tonight for sure."

As foreman of the Alaska Road Commission camp at Paxson, a wide spot in the Richardson Highway about 150 miles southeast of Fairbanks, Jerry was a sort of ambulatory newspaper for 20 or more roadhouse operators who, like myself, depended on highway traffic for a living. If he said visitors were on the way, I could believe it.

My place, Moochigan Lodge, sat on the edge of Summit Lake, a stone's throw from the highway and nine miles north of Jerry's homestead at Paxson.

"Why the sad face?" I asked. "After all, a little late-season business would be the next best thing to an early spring." I meant it, too. The summer of 1949 had come and gone like a running deer. Worse yet, it promised to be a long, cold winter.

"It's nobody you know," Jerry replied. "I'm talking about that old sow grizzly that's been raising cain around Paxson for the past couple of weeks. The one with the cub. You've probably heard about 'em already."

This was some of the best grizzly country in Alaska. We knew it and so did swarms of sportsmen who regularly made our lodge their hunting headquarters.

Here, the Richardson Highway bisected a panorama of low, brush-covered hills laced with blueberry thickets. Fishing was excellent in dozens of nearby lakes and streams. Annually, the caribou herds drifting past provided a ready source of meat for lean-bellied predators.

But a killing frost had denuded blueberry bushes for miles around in mid-August that year, and reports of marauding bears had been only too common. Indian summer had been frozen in its tracks, and the area's population of big game had grown hungrier and more ill-tempered with each passing week.

"Anyway," Jerry continued, "the sow and her cub have moved up to your neck of the woods, They're hungry, Dan. They've been prowling the old fish camps, and the sow's a big one. She's buffalo-colored and mean." A recital of the grizzly's depredations followed.

According to Jerry, the sow and her cub had been busier around Paxson than a colony of beavers. Garbage cans, ever a favorite target, had been ransacked nightly and a number of food caches violated.

It wasn't until Jerry told of actually being chased by the grizzly, however, that I became alarmed. With Maxine hanging on every word, he recounted an incident that had taken place the previous evening.

Dusk was coming on, and Jerry had been working in the clearing behind his cabin at the edge of the road commission camp. Suddenly, with no more warning than a sneeze, the sow had charged from a nearby clump of brush.

From her position on the back porch, the big fellow's wife screamed a warning. Jerry looked up, found himself cut off from the cabin, and legged it for the camp bunkhouse. He'd won the race by a whisker.

I digested the tale in silence, then shrugged in a poor attempt to conceal my misgivings. But Maxine wasn't fooled.

"I just thought of something " she exclaimed. "Dan killed a caribou last week. The meat is hanging outside the kitchen door right now, like an invitation to supper."

I had to grin, remembering the day not too many years before when I'd suggested to Maxine that she learn to hunt. Just then she was outguessing her teacher.

"And the wind, Dan," she continued excitedly. "It's been in the north since yesterday. The old sow is bound to have caught the scent. She'll be here about dark like Jerry says. Wait and see."

"Maybe," I said, "and maybe not. Anyhow, with this fresh snow on the ground the two of them shouldn't be hard to track."

Jerry nodded agreement. Without a word, Maxine crossed the room and plucked my .401 Winchester autoloader off its pegs. That model was discontinued in 1936, but I had mine rebuilt around 1939. If my wife was worried as she handed me the rifle, she didn't show it.

Throughout my 22 years in Alaska I'd killed my share of bears, and I guess Maxine had confidence in my ability. It still gets me when I realize how she was forced to revise her thinking before dark.

It was snowing lightly when Jerry and I left the roadhouse. We climbed into his pickup and headed south along Richardson Highway. I remember turning in my seat as we rounded the first curve. Maxine was waving good-bye from the roadhouse door.

"Last report I had," Jerry said, "the sow and her cub were poking around near Fish Creek. Might be a good place to start looking." Then, as an afterthought, "Dan, that old devil will go about 800 pounds, and she's just itching for trouble. How about postponing this deal? I'll take tomorrow off and we'll make a hunt of it."

I shook my head. Jerry's recent, narrow escape had convinced me of something that made killing the bear quickly imperative. It was my guess that the animal was nursing an old wound.

I told Jerry that in my opinion someone armed with a small-caliber rifle had taken a shot at the sow. As her wound festered, her temper had followed suit until she became hostile and constituted a real menace.

In all my years in Alaska, and while acting as a big-game guide, I'd never heard of a healthy bear charging a human being. As a rule, the average bear--any variety, any size--is sociable enough when left alone.

Though he'll go out of his way to keep your scent in the wild, the odds are long he's not looking for more than a nodding acquaintance. On occasion, I'd even run bears out of my way with rocks and sticks, or just an ear-splitting, banshee yell.

Though he shared my suspicions about the sow, Jerry made one last attempt to stall off my search. Again I rejected any delay. While he eased the truck through the snow, I strained my eyes for bear sign.

Funny, I thought, how a first snowfall can change the look of a countryside. Yesterday the brush had seemed visibly thin, like a blanket of twisted wire laid across the hills. Today, it was thickly padded with the white down payment of an early winter.

We'd gone a little over a mile when I signaled for a halt. Near the mouth of a small culvert that ran beneath the highway I'd spotted a welter of tracks.

"Could be some trucker stopped for water," Jerry said, "but let's have a look."

He pulled the truck off the road and we climbed out. From 20 feet away you could read the sign like a book. The footprints were big and comparatively fresh. The telltale cub tracks were right there beside the big ones. Following them toward the low ridge that paralleled the road would be easy.

I felt a surge of excitement as I climbed to the top of the pickup, and, between the intermittent flurries, scanned the white slope with my binoculars. I remembered other winters when I'd hunted and trapped these hills alone. Every dip and rise in the landscape was back-of-the-hand familiar.

Right now, however, my quarry was at least one ridge away. The glasses revealed no sign of life on the nearest hillside.

I jumped to the ground. Without a word, Jerry climbed into the truck, backed it farther off the highway, then pocketed the key.

"What's the big idea?" I asked.

He shrugged, and the wolfskin parka wrinkled comically around his neck.

"I'll climb to the top of the ridge with you and have a look around," he said. "Might see something moving on the other side."

The bears had broken a wide trail, and walking was easy. A light snow was still falling, and I judged the temperature to be a comfortable 10 degrees.

On the summit of the ridge we came across droppings to which the snow had already begun to adhere. This, and the amount of snow that had collected in the tracks, convinced us the sow and her cub had a good three-hour head start. Their trail angled slightly across the valley below, then rose again to the next low ridge about half a mile away.

By now, Jerry's conscience had begun to get the best of him. His road-clearing gang faced a long, tough day, and more snow was definitely on the way. With a final warning about watching my step, he waved good-bye and started back the way we had come. I continued on.

Within minutes, the snow began to thicken noticeably. An hour or two of this and the trail would be obliterated. I picked up the pace.

By now, however, something else had begun to disturb me. Beyond the shadow of a doubt, the sow and her offspring were headed for my lodge. Mentally, I projected their route. By nightfall, it would bring the pair to my back door and the ripening caribou meat that even now must be wafting its mouth-watering scent across the hills.

By the time I'd panted to the second ridgetop, the valley beyond was curtained completely by the snow. It fell in long, sullen waves from the lowering sky and all but hid the line of brush about 10 yards below the ridge crest where the tracks ended.

I stopped and thought the matter over carefully. The chances were good that a mile or more still separated me from the two grizzlies. The tracks were filling up. The snow made the binoculars useless, and plunging blindly into the brush was out of the question.

The sow was man-wise and mean. In all likelihood she was still traveling. On the other hand, she might have caught my scent and doubled back under cover of the storm to stalk me.

Later--while mulling things over in a hospital bed--I would conclude that this moment of hesitation probably saved my life. Had I turned back, the sow would have nailed me from behind, unseen. Plunging ahead would no doubt have proved equally fatal.

At any rate, I was standing there, cold and undecided--my binoculars in one hand, my rifle in the other--when the sow exploded like a four-footed thunder-clap from the line of brush not 30 feet away. Her deep-throated roar ripped through the silence on the ridge. Instinctively, I let the binoculars fall on the strap around my neck, swung my rifle in the grizzly's direction, and yanked the trigger. In the split second that should have preceded the blast, I glimpsed the sow's crazy red eyes and hair standing ramrod straight along her back. Then I experienced the sickest, most all-gone moment in my life.

For the first time since I'd bought the .401 back in 1932, the autoloader failed to fire. Instead of its usual, death-dealing bellow, the rifle responded to my trigger pull with a dry, harmless click. Desperately, I pumped another shell into the chamber just as 800 pounds of rock-hard, crazy-mad grizzly slammed me to the ground.

Luckily, my binoculars broke the force of the sow's first swipe. Despite the protection of the glasses and four or five layers of heavy clothing, her claws laid open my chest as neatly as a surgeon's knife--and I didn't feel a thing. As I staggered backward, I managed to crack the sow a solid blow on the nose with the butt of my rifle. She snapped viciously at the weapon, but I hung on. It was my only hope, and I knew it.

Then I was on the ground, and from my worm's-eye view the bear looked as big as a mountain. Methodically, she began making mincemeat of my left arm, and when I yelled in pain she snapped at my head.

In the years since, I've relived that moment 1,000 times in my dreams. Without fail, the memory of the grating sound the sow's teeth made across my skull is enough to awaken me in a cold sweat. And always I wake up kicking, just as I was kicking when it happened.

By now, though only a few seconds had elapsed since the bear struck me, I felt as if I'd been flat on my back for an eternity. And while I kicked and screamed and cursed, I kept thinking what a lousy way this was to die. I thought of Maxine and the kids--Maxine with another baby on the way and me in hock to my blood-soaked eyebrows. The more I thought of it the harder I kept digging my size 12 boots in the sow's belly.

Then, as if annoyed at the time it was taking to put me away, the grizzly bit through my face from the center of my nose to my right temple. The blurred image of her oncoming fangs was the last thing I ever saw through my right eye.

The pain inside my head mushroomed to killing proportions, and I fought frantically to retain consciousness. The temptation to drop my rifle and grab my head was almost overpowering. But I was staking my dwindling chances on the gun--and finally my opportunity came.

Annoyed at my incessant kicking, the sow, which had transferred her attentions from my head to my left leg, eventually backed off and grabbed my right leg above the offending boot. In that single, redeeming instant, I pointed the rifle at her broad chest and pulled the trigger.

I saw the hair blow straight up on the grizzly's back as 250 grains of lead crashed completely through her. She dropped my foot and reared upward a few inches, her forepaws off the ground. Her death roar and that of the rifle sounded almost as one. She flopped on her belly at my feet--lifeless.

I fell back in the snow. It seemed terribly quiet all of a sudden, though my ears still rang. Then the realization began to sink in. The bear was dead. I'd won. I was alive!

I said it over and over to myself, five, maybe six times. I couldn't believe my luck. Like a fighter on the verge of being knocked out, I'd thrown a desperation haymaker and connected.

A moment later, reality in the form of a 100-foot-high wall of pain put things back in sharp focus. When the spasm passed, I staggered to my feet.

Now that it was all over I was scared. Thank God, I thought, Maxine can't see me now.

I put my right hand on top of my head. My scalp was literally in ribbons, A large piece of skin was draped across my good eye, and I eased it upward gently. It promptly tumbled down again, triggering a fresh flow of blood. I ripped off what was left of my undershirt and wrapped it around my head. With only my right arm usable, it took a bit of doing.

The grizzly had given my left arm a thorough going over. I surveyed the mess impersonally, as if it belonged to someone else. One glance convinced me that even if I made it to a doctor, the shredded arm would have to come off.

As a souvenir of the blow that knocked me down, I had three deep claw cuts across my chest. I remember marveling at their neatness. Six inches higher and the swipe would have been fatal.

But it was my lacerated left leg that concerned me most. It was on fire with pain, and I faced a long hike back to the highway. Just above my left ankle the blood was pouring from a big hole where the bear had got in some of her final licks.

I cautiously shifted my weight to the leg. The bone appeared to be intact, but the movement was sheer agony. I groaned--both in pain and at the thought of the distance I had to travel.

Suddenly, I noticed I'd begun to shake. That's right, I thought, go ahead and panic--panic like a damned tenderfoot, out here in the middle of God-only-knows-where, and you've had it.

Then, from force of habit, perhaps, I leaned down to pick up my rifle. That was stupid. I awoke, probably only moments later, with my face buried in the snow, smothering.

That did it. Time was running out. I lurched to my feet, and, without so much as a backward glance at my dead attacker, went reeling down the trail.

My attention focused on only four things during the next terrible hour and a half. The first was a snappy debate with myself about the wisdom of taking a shortcut to the highway. I abandoned the notion quickly in favor of returning the way I'd come. At least one person knew the route I had taken and would look for me along the trail if I failed to show up.

117

And I recall seeing the brush move along the trail and imagining it was the cub. You're an orphan now, little guy, I said to myself. Old Man Winter will get you, sure as hell.

Next, somewhere along the way, I looked down at my right hand and saw it still clutched the rifle. Angrily, I flung it into a snowbank. Packing all that extra weight, I thought. How dumb can you get?

A pain-racked eternity later, I staggered onto the highway at the exact spot where I'd left it. Luck was with me.

As I slumped to the ground, a freight truck was braking to a stop at the culvert. The driver, Lewis Clarke, was an old friend.

While he loaded me into the cab I mumbled details of my scrap with the grizzly. Louie kept saying something that sounded like "Good God," and shaking his head. We finally got going north, in the direction of my lodge. I insisted we roll right past. I didn't want Maxine and the kids to see me like this. Anyway, the nearest doctor was at Big Delta Air Force Base 70 miles north, where the Richardson Highway joins the Alaska Highway.

The trip was a confused blur in my pain-occupied mind. I recall that we stopped at a roadhouse well beyond mine, and Louie passed the word ahead to the Army Alaska Arctic Training Center, which also occupied the base and ran the hospital. He called Maxine also and told her I'd been hurt. She promised to go at once to Fairbanks where I was eventually to be taken.

An Army ambulance met our truck some miles south of the Big Delta intersection. At the base I was given sedatives and first aid, then placed in another ambulance that headed for the hospital in Fairbanks in a blinding snowstorm.

In the 50 miles between the towns, the ambulance got stuck four times in king-size drifts. It was early evening before Dr. William Smith of the Fairbanks Medical and Surgical Clinic got me on his table.

In the hours that followed he took more than 200 stitches in my face, scalp, chest, arm, and leg. He managed to save the arm I'd given up for lost, and to reattach my ear. My right eye, however, was beyond repair.

Ten days later, I was bound for Seattle and a succession of operations spread out over a period of six months. I was fitted with a plastic right eye.

I've regained complete use of my injured arm and leg. The leg, by the way, gets a workout every morning. Immediately after rising I kick the head of a huge bear rug that decorates the floor of my bedroom.

Jerry Luebke made me a present of my ex-assailant's hide. The day after my epic one-rounder in the wilderness, he returned to the ridge, skinned out the grizzly, and recovered my rifle. As we suspected, the sow had been wounded once before--with a slug from a .25/20.

# 13

# NEVER TRUST A MOOSE

## By Eric Collier

## Outdoor Life, September 1953

*A bull moose weighs about 1,500 pounds and, typically, is not much of a threat. But moose are unpredictable and cranky. Find one that figures life owes him a stomping and you have trouble.*

*Eric Collier has always been a hero to me. Back in the 1920's, Collier took his family to remote British Columbia and built his cabin, where he stayed and raised his family for many years.*

*Collier wrote of his adventures in Three Against The Wilderness, a wonderful adventure of a man and his family on a new frontier. Here is a story he wrote about Old Cantankerous, a moose who tried to change the Collier neighborhood.*

I should have known better in the first place. I was hunting mule deer in a tongue of fir and lodgepole pine forest that licks almost at the log walls of our home in the British Columbia wilderness, where I farm beavers and muskrats in their natural habitat. A November moon was waning, and three inches of snow blanketed the kinnikinnick and blueberry vines. The wind was faintly from the Arctic, the air tangy and crisp with a definite hint of more snow to come.

Now was the time I must go to work and stock our moss-chinked meat house against the hungry months ahead. In my country a deer killed in November stays frozen until the following April.

I found my buck--a three-pointer--bedded on the rim of a deep gulch, staring languidly into the westering sun, as bucks have been doing on late-November afternoons ever since there have been bucks. I shot him in his bed, dragged him out of the gulch, and gutted him. Then I put him beneath a fir tree to cool off. Next morning I'd come with a horse and pack him to the meat house. Standing beside the steaming carcass, 30 yards from the rim of the gulch, I could neither see nor hear any movement below. True, a red squirrel shucked a cone from a fir tree, but squirrels don't count. Yet I had a sudden intuition that life was abroad down there in the bowels of the gulch, although why I don't know. But it was definitely there, and I bolted a cartridge into the breech of my .303 Ross, crouched back on my heels, and strained my ears and eyes.

A bull moose of full maturity weighs around 1,400 pounds on the hoof, and he may carry a rack of horns spreading 60 inches or better. It doesn't seem possible that so large an animal can move through timber as silently as a foraging lynx cat. But it can, and it does; a bull moose is often seen before it's heard.

Such was the case that afternoon. The horns came up out of the gulch first; a spread of 45 inches, I judged. Then the grotesque Roman nose, followed by the rest of the head. It was the kind of opportunity a trophy hunter dreams about but doesn't often get.

I wasn't interested in trophies, for I have yet to find horns that taste good in a stew. At the moment I wasn't even interested in moose. I don't like their meat, for I ate far too much of it during the gaunt years of the depression. And I'd left my camera at home.

It was a couple of seconds before horns, head, body and all four legs were up out of the gulch. Then, head high and nostrils testing the air, the bull moved stiffly toward me. That was odd, for he could see me crouching tensely by the body of the deer. By all rules of the game he should have wheeled and gone back into the gulch much more quickly than he'd left it. But he moved up to within 20 yards before he stopped and gazed at me intently, obviously unafraid. If I've ever seen mayhem in a bull moose's eyes, it was in his.

For 33 straight years my everyday life has been spent here, and these woods had to provide me not only with a living but with recreation to boot. After all, when you're 100-odd miles from the nearest electric light you wouldn't recognize Clark Gable if you met him along the trail.

Anyway I'd think twice before digging into my jeans for the price of a movie ticket. But I'll spend hours in the hush of the forest, crooning softly to a suspicious bull moose, inching up, camera ready to snap a picture if I can get within 15 to 20 feet before he takes off. That's my personal moose hunting. I do it with a rather poor camera but if you don't like an animal's meat or want a trophy why hunt him with a gun?

Sure, I guide moose hunters in the fall, but my job is to find the bull; they take over from there.

I've been within 15 to 20 feet of more moose than I can tell you about--and got photos of almost every one--but up to the time of this story I'd yet to shoot my first bull or cow in self-defense. Several had got snooty enough, for if you work around a moose any considerable time it soon sheds its instinctive fear and distrust and begins talking back. When that happens you start looking at your hole card.

When a cow or bull has fight on its mind, there's a lot in its expression that isn't altogether sweet. The ears flatten against the neck, the mane stands up, and the whites of the eyes show. Usually there's only a single soft grunt of warning, and then the animal moves forward and comes exceedingly fast. That's why I brought the .303 to my shoulder within a split second of the big bull's first show of truculence. Maybe I should have settled the business for good right then and there, and been spared the ordeal that was to come.

I know now that I'd have been forced to shoot if a yearling hadn't got into the act, because here was one moose that would kill or be killed. But the yearling temporarily solved the problem, paying a harsh price for doing so. I didn't know he was around until the bull suddenly pulled his eyes from me to stare questioningly and belligerently at something off in the timber.

I lowered my rifle and followed the line of this stare. At first I could see nothing except timber, but after another prolonged look I saw a yearling bull moving slowly toward the gulch. The little fellow wasn't doing any harm; just nipping the shoot of a red willow here, or rubbing his poor sprout of horns against a seedling fir there.

Feeding slowly toward us, he apparently didn't notice the big bull until he was within 30 yards of him. Then he tossed up his head and froze in his tracks. Somehow I wanted to yell, "Get the blazes out of here, you little fool, while the getting is good!" But it wouldn't have helped.

The yearling was oozing good nature, and it was as clear as the air you breathe that he just wanted to move up alongside the big bull and pass the time of day. As he started forward again I heard the big boy grunt. There was a weight of hidden warning in that grunt to anyone who understands moose talk. Again I was tempted to shoot but I couldn't make up my mind to. The old bull charged before I could decide.

Despite popular belief, a bull moose does far more fighting with his front feet than with his horns. True, the antlers are used extensively, and sometimes with fatal effect when the heat of the rut is on. But at any other time of year it is the front quarters that throw the most lethal blows.

That yearling was worse off than any babe in the woods. By the time he came awake to what it was all about the big bull was almost within striking range. Then the youngster did something you'll not often see a sensible moose do. He wheeled and broke into a gallop. And a galloping moose is about as graceful as a knock-kneed man in a sack race.

I didn't even see the first blow, it flicked out so fast. But I certainly heard it connect. Crack! A sickening crack, too--one that could be heard from one end of the gulch to the other. The youngster stumbled and almost went down. Crack! I saw it this time. It was like the flick of a swamp adder's head. And the little fellow was down in the snow.

That's when I roared in instinctive anger. The right-front foot of the big bull was raised for another blow, but at the sound of my voice it went stiffly back into the snow. The bull half turned, staring angrily at me. Thus the yearling got his one chance for a getaway, and he lost no time grabbing it. Limping badly--I'm sure his hip had been dislocated--he came up from the snow and lurched away into the sanctuary of the gulch.

The bull moose continued his belligerent appraisal of me for a moment. Then he blew his nostrils, scratched vigorously at his right ear with his hind foot, shook himself, and moved slowly off into the thickets.

"You cantankerous old bum!" I yelled after him.

Old Cantankerous was as good a name as any for him, and he lived up to every syllable of it.

In my country moose browse the timbered ridges until the snow sets knee-deep, then come down to the beaver dams and pasture in the second-growth beaver cuttings. Usually this is not until Christmas or New Year, but that year Mother Nature showed the harsher side of her breasts, and by December 15 the snow was belly-deep to a calf, and the moose came drifting into the creek bottom. Old Cantankerous was among them.

I was kneeling down building myself a mink set in the overflow of a beaver dam, and at first glance I didn't fully recognize him, although I knew I'd seen this bull somewhere before. He'd shed his horns, and that made a difference.

He was standing on the ice of the beaver pond 50 yards upstream, and had neither seen nor winded me. A beaver dam covered with sodden snow is exceedingly treacherous footing, and my snowshoes were on the far side of it, 300 feet or so away. So was my Boss .303. When I finally recognized the bull, I cursed myself and began fruitlessly scheming how I could get across to the rifle without attracting his attention. But I decided it would be better to stay put until he moved off. I think I was scared of that bull.

I cautiously sank down behind the dam, wishing he'd go so I could finish my business. I wasn't looking for trouble that afternoon. After at least 15 minutes of indecision he smelled the snow, belched, and veered up-pond toward a willow patch that would furnish his supper.

Christmas sulked in on a bloated full moon. Azure skies, and a wind out of the Yukon as sharp as porcupine needles. Spruce trees along the creek bottoms popping their useless protests. A little cross fox yapping on a mountaintop, beseeching the harsh land that had spawned him to give him food. Moose calves coming up from their beds in the snow at daybreak, with frosted hocks and ears; chickadees falling from the perches in the spruce thickets, little feathered bodies frozen solid while they roosted. Christmas, the birthday of our Lord; Christmas and 54 degrees below zero.

You don't trap mink, otters, or other fur bearers in weather like that; only the coyotes and timber wolves are abroad. And moose. Come rip-roaring chinook or searing Arctic blizzard, moose must eat. The lower the mercury, the more browse they must consume lest the body heat be extinguished within them. No shed or den for them; just the overhang of a spruce tree for shelter, virgin snow for a bed.

For myself, hibernating over a potbellied stove soon becomes irksome. Two or three days of it is all my stomach can stand. Then, cold or no cold, I must busy myself with some outdoor chore. While the cold snap lasted, running the traplines would be a dreary, useless business, So, having mastered the somewhat tricky art of handling a camera with mittens, I went to stalking moose. And by moose I mean Old Cantankerous.

And that brought me to New Year's Day. Thirty-six inches of snow, now, and warmer. Only 28 below. Gray, scurfy clouds scudding across the face of the sun: mink tracks again beginning to show in the seepage from the beaver dams. For that's another miracle of the beaver. No matter how bitter the cold, the water seeps through his dams and moves freely down the creek to keep its rendezvous with the river.

That afternoon the bull chewed his cud at the edge of a small meadow only half a mile from my cabin, and my mind was made up. I'd get a photograph. But now there was a nasty question that had to be solved. How could I handle camera and rifle at the same time? No matter how quick you are, it takes a second or two to drop the camera, unsling the gun, slip the safety, and bring the butt to your shoulder. A mature bull moose, murder in his eye, covers a deal of ground in just two or three seconds. I wasn't kidding myself; if Old Cantankerous were to charge, only powder and lead would stop him.

Had my son been at home the whole affair would have been simple. He'd cover the bull while I took the photo. But he wasn't with us. The previous fall he'd traded the loneliness of the wilderness for a three-year hitch in the Canadian army. That day there was only my wife.

I broached the matter quite casually. "I believe we could get a picture of Old Cantankerous this afternoon," I told her. She knew all about him by this time and was under no illusion as to what I meant by "getting a picture." It meant stalking to within 10 or 15 feet of the big bull.

"We?"

"If you'd like to handle the camera while I cover with the gun?" I said, a little tolerantly. Perhaps I was hoping she'd say, "You couldn't get me within 400 yards of that brute!" Then maybe I'd have scuttled the whole idea.

Instead, she began pulling on her overshoes in a very matter-of-fact way. Which is what I should have expected, for we came into the wilderness together determined to enjoy the sunshine and endure the storm. Why should I think she'd deny me when I asked that she share my adventures with a moose?

While she was piling on sweaters and mackinaw I got her snowshoes from a shed and pummeled the leather harness soft. Next we checked the box camera. It held four unused negatives. I took the .303 Ross down from its peg on the wall and fondled it briefly, for that old gun has been with me since 1922.

"Ready?" I asked my wife. She was set to go, all 115 pounds of her, and seemed impatient to get this bit of business over with. I stared thoughtfully at the five 220-grain soft-points in the palm of my hand and hoped I wouldn't have to use one. I dropped the cartridges into the magazine and stepped into my snowshoes. "O.K.," I said.

A smooth trapping trail took us within 100 yards of the meadow. The bull hadn't moved; he was still out in the open, 15 yards from the brush. He half turned in his tracks as we came into view, watching us with seeming indifference. The approach across the meadow wasn't easy, for here the snow was 36 inches deep. Our snowshoes sank into it for some eight or 10 inches, and each time we lifted a foot three pounds of snow came up on the webbing.

"Think you can manage it?" I asked.

"I think so," my wife said.

With me breaking trail, we moved cautiously to within 30 yards of the bull. He looked as big as a mountain, and he was watching us with bold intentness. I stopped and slid a shell into the breech of the .303 and pulled the moose-hide mitten from my right hand. Now there was just a thin woolen glove between my finger and the trigger. I stared at the old bull. As long as he stood with his ears well up and his mane down we had nothing to fear.

We slid forward again and now there was only 15 yards between us and the bull. I stopped and breathed, "How does he look through the finder?"

"I'll try one but another five yards would be better."

Another five yards! That would put her within 10 yards of a bull moose packing as much danger as a case of ditching powder. I was beginning to experience a gnawing uneasiness.

"Unbuckle the heelstraps of your snowshoes," I suddenly told her. Free of the straps she could still move forward, but, in an emergency, could slip quickly out of the shoes and dodge. She unbuckled the straps and looked up at me. "O.K.," I said. "Another five yards--but not an inch closer."

We never made it. The words had hardly left my mouth when I heard the old bull grunt. Both his ears flattened back against his neck, his mane bristled over his withers, and his eyes rolled to show a bloodshot white.

I sucked in my breath. "Quick--shoot now!" I said.

The camera came up against her chest and she looked down into the finder just as the old bull charged. A scream forced itself from her lips, "You shoot!" she cried.

Even in the flick of time it took for the gun to jump to my shoulder, for my eye to look down the sights, he was almost on top of her. It had to be a brain shot; no other could possibly drop him before his front feet began pounding my wife to a pulp. A good many thoughts might have hammered at my brain in the moment. I might have been cursing myself for exposing her to this danger in the first place. I might have thought of the 100-mile trek with sleigh and team to a doctor.

But there was only one thought, and it was more of a prayer: that the .303 wouldn't miss. I held my fire deliberately since there would be no time to reload. Somehow I managed to keep the pressure off that trigger until he was 10 measured feet from her snowshoes. Then I held right between his eyes and tripped the trigger of the Ross. A brain shot, I'd said. It had to be a brain shot. And, thank God, a brain shot it was. He was dead when he hit the snow.

Slowly, almost reluctantly, my eyes rose to meet those of my wife. The fear that had been in her lingered in the tenseness of her face, the pallor of her cheeks, the dilated pupils of her eyes. And it was a fear of which she need never feel shame. To see Old Cantankerous standing and chewing his cud would tingle the roots of your hair; to see him charging was a vision of hell itself.

I looked down at his body, still quivering in death. My thoughts went back to the gulch and the yearling, to those other moose he had quarreled with as they approached his reeding spot.

I thought of the long winter days ahead when I'd be away from home on some distant part of the trapline, and my wife there alone. True, I had killed a bull moose out of lawful season, and while game laws are necessary to the preservation of wildlife, there are isolated occasions when breaking them does far more good than harm.

My wife had rebuckled the heelstraps of her snowshoes and started toward me when a thought flashed through my mind. I held up my hand. "Wait," I said. "I want a photo of you right there where you were when he went down."

I moved forward, took the camera from her, and backed up a couple of snowshoe lengths. I was about to take the picture when she asked, "Did you wind it?"

"Wind it!" I almost shouted. And as the words sank in, I asked in amazement, "You mean there's a photo of him charging?"

"I think so," she said.

There are a good many things in the life of one who follows the forests and watersheds for a living that I cannot properly explain. How she was able to keep her eyes on the camera, hold the thing steady, and press the button when 1,400 pounds of rage was almost on top of her is one of them.

# 14

# HOW TO STOP AN ELEPHANT

### By John Taylor

### Pondoro: Last of the Ivory Hunters

### Simon & Schuster, 1955

*The real danger from elephants, claims professional hunter John Taylor, is from the big bulls that you don't see. You have your eye on one animal and a bull suddenly charges from the side or behind you...and you never knew he was there. This gray bellowing mountain is suddenly on top of you and you've got to stop him with a small bullet. If you fail, there won't be much left of you to send home.*

*In a different time, there were plenty of elephants. Progress and poachers had not yet taken their toll. Hunting these glorious animals did little to reduce their numbers. A handful of professional hunters excelled at elephant hunting because of their courage and knowledge of the animal's anatomy. Two such men were John Taylor and Karamojo Bell. Here are the classic tales of their hunts long past.*

You don't have to be a crack shot to be a successful elephant hunter--a very mediocre marksman can still kill elephant. I do not pretend to be any Deadeye Dick or lay claim to any fancy degree of marksmanship; yet I kill nearly all my elephant with a single shot apiece. That is not necessarily superlative skill. It is just that I do not get all steamed up; I do not attempt to squeeze the trigger until I am certain of at least anchoring my beast--no matter what it is--if not instantly killing it. Steadiness and patience are of much greater importance than actual marksmanship. After all, you must have noticed that most elephant are shot within 25 yards and that I refer to 40 yards as a very long shot. So it is, at elephant.

ʏ In the Asenga country the grass is the trouble. There are oceans of 10- to 12-foot elephant grass, and the herds seem to spend most of their time in it. I have heard it described as maddening. But there are swarms of elephant there in the right season.

When I got into the Asenga country the thought that instantly jumped into my mind was: Now if only I had a kind of house decorator's ladder, how easy it would be. Why I should have thought of that particular type of ladder I don't know--I've never been a house decorator myself, nor used such a ladder. But there it was. Moreover, there was plenty of bamboo growing in the district, so it was a fairly simple matter to make a usable ladder--though its not having any hinges made it a somewhat rickety affair. Still, with the two men who carried it steadying it when I climbed to the top, it was quite practical. I used it with great success. But I considered it preferable to use a small-bore rifle rather than one of my more powerful weapons because I was afraid the latter might send me flying from my perch on the top of the ladder if the fellows who were supposed to be steadying it got bored with the proceedings, as they almost inevitably would when the shooting had been going on for some time and they were unable to see what was happening; and also because I found that the elephant were not alarmed by the report of the small rifle to the extent they were by the heavier one. Sitting on top of the ladder with my shoulders just level with the tops of the grass I would wait for an elephant to raise his head sufficiently or move into a place where the grass had been trampled down a bit. Then it was merely a case of slipping the little slug into his brain. He would drop instantly and disappear in the grass-- there wouldn't be a sound out of him. Consequently, his pals wouldn't know that anything had happened to him: because they couldn't see him fall on account of the grass, and because there was no commotion to alarm them, the whiplike crack of the small-bore being something they hadn't heard before. I have shot as many as seven like that without having to move my ladder; and then about half an hour later killed another five out of the same herd from a different position. The principal difficulty I experienced when using this method was to decide if an elephant were worth shooting or not. Frequently I would get only a fleeting glimpse of his tusks; sometimes I could not even get that.

I picked up the spoor of a pretty big herd in Rhodesia and followed them over the Tanganyika border when they crossed. I caught up with them in one of those places you dream about with everything in your favor: There was a fair-sized clearing in the light, open forest with a mud wallow in the middle of it and a couple of dusting places close by. Halfway between the fringe of the forest and the mud wallow was a small anthill with a couple of forked trees growing out of it. These afforded adequate cover for me and my gunbearer, for the trees broke up our outline--making us invisible provided we kept still--yet in no way interfered with our view of the herd or impeded quick handling and exchange of rifles. An ideal spot. The anthill was perhaps 40 paces from the mud wallow and 20 to 30 paces from the two dusting places.

We sighted the herd when we were fully 150 yards away. The elephant were thoroughly enjoying themselves; slapping dollops of mud onto their shoulders and backs with a satisfying clop, as happy as children making mud pies; others, having had their mud baths, were scraping the bare ground of the dusting places with one huge forefoot, then sucking up a trunkful of the dust and puffing it over heads, necks, shoulders, and behind huge ears, for all the world like women completing their toilet. One very big bull, which I guessed was the leader, had had his bath and shampoo and was now doing nothing under the trees. All this reminded me of a veritable "elephant playground" I had once found in a district to the north of the Zambezi. I had been hunting with but moderate success for some three or four weeks and was wondering to myself which of all the various districts known to me would be the best right now. I knew I ought to be doing better and would do better if I could just hit upon the right district. Having made up my mind, I decided to give this section one more day. I had noticed a large circular patch of extraordinarily dense bush with a good deal of heavy timber growing in it. Elephant paths led toward it, but so far I hadn't had occasion to examine it. Each time I passed that way I was following spoor which did not lead directly into it. I now decided to have a look at the place and see what it was like inside. But the local natives were horrified at the idea of entering. They declared the place was haunted--though they didn't know by what-- and that anyway the elephant would certainly kill any human being who was foolish enough to enter. When I told them I had every intention of entering, they did everything in their power to try to dissuade me. They were really concerned about it. This one sent for that one, and he sent for someone else, until I had all the elders of the district around me. They told me what they thought were horrifying tales of the savagery of the elephant if their chosen playgrounds were ever violated by man. They assured me that elephant which might well be afraid of me and my rifles elsewhere would be very different animals if I attempted to look for them in their playground.

I didn't doubt there was a good deal of truth in what they said; but nevertheless I wasn't worried. The elephant could be as savage as they liked, but their savagery wouldn't be a match for my fine rifles--at least I hoped it wouldn't. It would all depend on the type of bush I found inside. If the place were, as the local men said, a kind of playground, then I had a hunch I would find it open once I succeeded in getting through the outer ring of bush.

But that same outer ring was an extremely nasty proposition when I came to tackle it. In all my wanderings only once or twice have I come across anything quite like it. I was following an elephant path which led directly toward it, but when I came to enter I found that the bush--not thorn--was as thick and dense as a box hedge which has been allowed to grow wild. It was utterly impenetrable except along the zigzag tracks made by the elephant themselves. The bush was about 15 feet high, and I found that I would have to get down on hands and knees to get along the little tunnel which was all that could be seen of the "path" because the bush closed up entirely from a height of about three feet up. The big gray beasts could brush through this as easily as I could brush through a field of wheat; but a man could not. I had a look at one or two other entrances, but they were all the same.

When I signified that I was about to enter the local men again tried to dissuade me, and when they saw that I wasn't listening to them they flatly refused to take another step. They said they would wait under a shady tree, but that they never expected to see me again. I asked my two gunbearers if they were coming with me or if they would rather wait outside. Their snorts of disgust at the notion that they should wait in safety while I went forward alone were masterpieces. Nevertheless, it wouldn't do to be careless. These local men weren't cowardly and there was no doubt about their fear; I had a hunch it wasn't all bugaboo. Moreover, we'd look pretty foolish if we met a herd coming our way as we crawled along on hands and knees trying not to let the muzzles of the rifles pick up sand.

In fact, I didn't entirely like it. True, there wasn't much likelihood of our meeting elephant coming our way at that hour; but it was pure surmise on my part that we were going to find better going ahead. For all I knew to the contrary there might be only an occasional small clearing around some of the larger trees. But having once started it was obviously out of the question to turn back--I just had to see what was in front.

We crawled along, swearing and dripping with sweat from every pore, for what seemed like two or three ages. And then suddenly, and without the slightest warning, we found ourselves on the edge of what looked like an old English park that had gone to seed a bit. Only in place of the few scattered deer that you would have seen once upon a time in an English park, here elephant were scattered about. Just elephant and nothing else. The dense bush had ceased as abruptly as it had begun. It must have been about 150 yards thick--though we had zigzagged much father than that--and looked for all the world as though it had been planted around that park the way a hedge is planted around a garden. But this hedge had never known a gardener's shears or clippers.

There were great shady trees here and there and small clumps of evergreen bush, and away down in the center we later found a spring of cool water gushing out between two large boulders. It ran into a deep clear pool which the elephant used for drinking purposes, and then into a few shallow pools which they used for mud baths. There were dusting places close by and, as we afterward discovered, salt licks also. It was a delightful place, and completely private. The short green grass almost deserved the name "sward"-- at least at first glance.

There were elephant drowsing under the trees, others drinking and blowing water over themselves, and cows washing down their youngsters; others again were slapping mud on themselves or powdering themselves with dust. All were perfectly happy and right out in the open. They obviously assumed they were quite safe in here. It seemed a shame to violate the peace of the place; yet one day's shooting wouldn't do much harm, and it might be many years before I visited it again.

There were not so many elephant, probably not more than 40 to 50, altogether. But it seemed as if there were many more because they were all over the place and right out in the open in a way you seldom see them nowadays except, perhaps, in some national park where they never hear a rifle speak. The glade seemed full of elephant. It was roughly circular and perhaps a quarter of a mile across.

We moved quietly around to our left, keeping close to the hedge, and so up along it to a spot where I could see two big tuskers under a shady tree. They were about 75 yards from the hedge, and there was a fair-sized anthill with a small bush growing out of the top of it roughly halfway between them and the hedge. I made for it. Taking up a position on top of the anthill, with the little bush to break up our outline, I opened fire. The two bulls collapsed in their tracks, and I reloaded the .400 myself instead of exchanging rifles, since no quick third shot was called for. The commotion that now ensued among the other elephant was truly remarkable; I have never seen anything quite like it. Some of them twisted and turned, this way and that, trying to spot the danger zone; others rushed here and there, trumpeting and screaming and adding to the general confusion. We stood quite still and watched them. There was one big old cow that appeared to be the leader of about a dozen other cows with a few half-grown calves among them and two or three immature bulls. I didn't at all like the purposeful manner in which she was looking for us. There was no indication of panic about her; on the contrary, she set out to find us in the most deliberate and reasoned way, her companions following her. These old cows are sometimes very dangerous. Since the lincensee never shoots them, long years of immunity give them an utter contempt for man, and it is by no means uncommon for them to kill the wretched owners of the "lands" when they go raiding and those owners try to drive them away. This old girl led her party right up to the two dead bulls and sniffed over them. Getting a whiff of the freshly spilled blood she suddenly wheeled around and loosed a shrill trumpeting blast. The result was extraordinary: every elephant in the glade suddenly froze in its tracks. There wasn't a sound or a movement.

Then slowly and quietly the old cow began to circle, her trunk snaking about, trying to pick up our wind. I declare she appeared to be tiptoeing. For a moment her companions remained still, then commenced to follow her. They circled to within about 25 yards of us, and it was quite obvious that it was only a matter time before the old cow got our wind. It was equally obvious that she would then charge. I really ought to have shot her then and there and been done with it; but I hated to fire if I could avoid it because there were several other shootable bulls in sight and I didn't want to stampede them if I could help it. But since a charge was so imminent,

I might just as well have dropped her without waiting for it. Possibly, I was interested in watching her methods. Naturally I had kept turning to face the cow, meaning that my two gunbearers also had to move to be always in their correct positions; and just before she was due to get our wind, the old cow suddenly wheeled around and with a scream of rage came bald-headed for us. She must have seen some slight movement back over her shoulder in the way elephant can without your knowing they are looking at you at all--like hogs.

With her ears back she looked incredibly vicious. As she came, her party came too. I had no alternative but to drop her. My little Purdey brought her down without any fuss, and with one exception those with her halted. The exception proved to be another big old cow who, trumpeting shrilly, endeavored to press home the charge. However, my left barrel took her between the eyes. Exchanging rifles, I waited. For what seemed a very long time the other members of the troop just stood about, ears cocked and trunks up, unable to make up their minds what to do. I did not want to turn my back and walk away, for that might well have provoked another charge, and I certainly didn't want to waste any more ammunition on them. But these two shots had started the ball rolling again among the other elephant in the glade. They trumpeted and yelled and rushed around but didn't seem to get anywhere. No attempt was made by any of them to clear out of the glade, though there was nothing to prevent their going. Never have I seen elephant so excited. At long last the troop of cows in front of me wheeled and dashed off for perhaps 100 yards or so, and then halted again.

I once more took over the little .400, since it looked as though anything could happen here. There was a good bull standing all by himself about 120 yards away, and a convenient tree within some 30 to 35 paces of him. I decided to make for it. We had to cross the open to get there and would be pretty nearly in the middle of the glade when we did so. I got the tree between him and myself and signed to my men to walk in single file behind me. We had no difficulty in getting to the tree without the big fellow's seeing us. However, I noticed that at least two other tuskers had spotted us, though they did not seem to realize what we were. They had seen something moving, something that wasn't an elephant, and their suspicions were aroused. One of them started slowly toward us with his ears out but his trunk down; the other stood there, ears cocked and trunk up, staring hard and trying to make out what it was. There were about 80 or 90 yards between them: one of them; one of them out on our right about 75 paces away, and the other beyond the one we were stalking, and also some 75 yards away. I slipped up behind the tree, edged around it, and let drive. My bull dropped dead without ever knowing that a rifle had been fired. With the other two bulls so threatening, I immediately exchanged rifles. The one on my right rolled up his trunk and came on the heels of the shot. But his rush appeared to be somewhat halfhearted. He wasn't roaring, and he didn't seem to be coming at full speed. The other certainly meant business. However, he didn't start quite so soon. In fact, he didn't start until he saw the other one coming. He made up for lost time then; but I decided to take the one on my right first as I felt pretty certain that the carcass of the first bull, almost directly in his path, would prove disconcerting. Whether the one on my right was really charging or merely bluffing, I cannot say. Anyhow, I dared not take a chance--besides, he was well worth shooting. My bullet took him, too, between the eyes and, without waiting to see the result, I instantly swung on the second. As I did so he reached the body of the earlier kill and immediately lost all interest in me. His trunk, which he had rolled up under his chin, he flung up over his head. He made a frantic effort to slew around. As he must have been coming at around 25 miles an hour he had to heel well over to make the sharp turn he wanted. My left barrel took him through the shoulder before he had completed the turn and literally blasted him off his feet-- there was no question about his charging. He had loosed the charging bull elephant's characteristic series of short roars--a tremendous volume of sound--up to the time he encountered the first dead elephant; the other hadn't made a sound of any sort.

I again exchanged rifles, for there was no telling what was going to happen now. The various other elephant seemed to go crazy, stark staring mad when they heard this shooting and heard the roars of the charging bull. One big fellow with only one tusk stood there blowing a long-sustained blast through his trunk. The others dashed madly around in the most senseless manner. One party came rushing straight toward us as though they intended to run us down. There didn't seem to be a really shootable beast among them, so I let them come on until they were about 30 to 40 yards away in the hope that they would pass. When it looked as though they were really coming over us, I raised the rifle with the intention of dropping the two leaders, because that would probably cause the rest to halt or swing outward. But it was not necessary to shoot. As my finger tightened on the trigger, of their own accord they pulled up and stood there staring at us. Then just as suddenly they wheeled around and dashed away again. We looked at each other with raised eyebrows, shrugged a shoulder, and grinned. We had had many strange experiences together, but today's performance beat anything we had ever seen.

I decided I would like to add that big old single-tusker to the bag. If I could get him I would be willing to call it a day. He was about 120 paces away standing broadside-on to me. It was an incredibly long shot at elephant; but I could get a beautifully steady shot from where I stood, and since there were several other beasts that would make a closer approach to the single-tusker difficult, I decided to have a try at him. My bullet shot him through the shoulder and there was no need for a second. The other elephant in the immediate vicinity cleared, thereby enabling us to wander around and collect the tails of the slain. But those elephant farther off wouldn't go. They stood watching us as we went from one carcass to another. Every now and then one of them would take a step or two toward us but would not attempt to interfere with us. They had quieted after the shot that killed the last, the old single-tusker; but it was most unusual for them just to stand around like that in the open and not make the slightest attempt to clear out of the vicinity. There were some of them within 60 to 70 yards of us the whole time, until we came to make our way out of the glade. I acted as rearguard then, and just before I started to crawl I looked back and saw the elephant still standing where we had left them.

As we emerged from the hedge the local natives, who had been sitting under a shady tree listening to the shooting and trumpeting, came racing up to hear our news. They could scarcely believe their eyes when they saw we were all in one piece and had actually to handle the tails of the dead elephant before they could be convinced they were real and not figments of the imagination. They assured one another I must possess some powerful spell, magic, medicine. How otherwise could I have emerged alive? The thing was almost unbelievable-- entirely unbelievable if it hadn't been for those freshly severed tails. They looked with genuine awe and admiration and respect at my two staunch gunbearers and pondered on the strength of my "medicine" that was sufficient to cover all three of us. This morning's work would be something to talk over for the next quarter century.

Whenever elephant hunters foregather and the conversation turns, as it inevitably will, to rifles, sooner or later someone will mention the great Karamojo Bell's name and refer to his phenomenal success with his beloved little 7mm Rigby-Mauser. (Bell's total bag amounted to 1,011 elephant, 800 killed with the 7mm and some 200 with the .303 British.)

Time and again I have heard men declare that what one man can do can be done again: that Bell may have had, indeed must have had, physique and stamina above the average; nevertheless he was human and if he could slay large numbers of elephant and make a handsome fortune for himself with a small-bore rifle why shouldn't the speaker be able to do it also, provided he could get himself an unrestricted permit? I repeat, I have heard this said on numerous occasions; and although Bell's original book, "The Wanderings of an Elephant Hunter," has long been out of print, his "Karamojo Safari" is still widely read, and I haven't the least doubt that many readers of it are asking the same question as that quoted above. In fact, I have myself received more than one inquiry in this connection. And the answer, of course, is easy: If the inquirer could put the clock back half a century or so, if he were as keen as Bell and as fit, and, most important, an equally fine marksman, then, if he hunted the same districts as Bell hunted and could win for himself the confidence and friendship and help of the local natives to the extent that Bell did, why, there is no very good reason why he shouldn't do as well as Bell did. But that if is a mighty big one.

You do not find mobs of old bull elephant right out in the open nowadays feeding and enjoying mud baths in broad daylight as Bell found them--remember, he was the very first man among those elephant, and it was mighty seldom he lost a pricked or wounded elephant. It is true that he did occasionally hunt and kill in heavy forest, but it was lone bulls or pairs of bulls he was following. Not once does he mention tackling mixed herds with nervous cows and their young calves under such conditions. And although it is customary to speak of those elderly bulls as "having tempers in inverse ratio to the length of their tusks," and even Bell himself does so, with all due respect to the man I have always ranked as the greatest elephant hunter of all time, that is hyperbole. My experience has been that the aged, whether elephant or man, are not looking for trouble: All they seek is peace and quiet. There is comparatively little danger in hunting lone bulls or pairs of bulls provided you go about it the right way. Why, in my younger days I was advised to let the herds alone and hunt only lone bulls. (That I did not follow the advice is another story.) When Bell shot mixed herds, he did so in open-grass country where he could see if a cow's charge was meant or merely fluff.

It cannot be seriously disputed that Bell's skill with the rifle was far above that of the average hunter. He admits that his marksmanship was of an "automatic accuracy" in those days, and that when he was shooting at fast-moving birds or elephant "the conscious section of mind allowed the rifle a certain amount of lead, but the instant the projectile was started on its way the subconscious section took charge, corrected the rifle, almost in a forward direction, and a clean kill would result. It was only when the subconscious aimer was not functioning that a miss would result. I caught but a fleeting glimpse of a disappearing stern. I succeeded in introducing a nicely judged bullet which, but for the above-mentioned subconscious aimer, would have passed harmlessly beneath the bound lion. The correction in this case was high, with the result that he was caught on the spine just abaft the shoulders while on the rise."

Well, I don't know how many hunters or sportsmen can claim such adventitious aid to their marksmanship. I wish I could! Bell, I consider, was one of those outstanding marksmen only one or two of which appear in a generation. The late Annie Oakley was just about at the peak of her career when Bell was starting out on his, and had he been a man of different caliber and concentrated on trick shooting instead of elephant, he might well have become a serious rival to Little Sure-Shot herself.

But the point I wish to make is that when tackling mixed herds in dense bush, as one has to nowadays if one wishes the bag to grow, circumstances can and sometimes do arise in which the greatest marksman who ever lived could not be sure of extricating himself if armed with a small-bore rifle. These occasions are not frequent but they must not be overlooked or forgotten: I have experienced them myself on several safaris and both know personally and have heard and read of several other hunters also experiencing them. Those who were armed with small-bores were either killed or it's not necessarily the elephant at which you're firing that constitutes the danger: the real danger may suddenly appear from some entirely unexpected direction and be right beside you before you have the remotest notion of its existence. It may have been there right along on the other side of a thick bush within trunk reach of you without your knowing.

There is another very important point to remember, and that is that the greatest marksmen will occasionally misplace his shot. It may not occur very often, but where elephant in thick cover and small-bore rifles are concerned, it doesn't have to occur more than once!

Bell describes a hunt in West Africa. Not having hunted since before the war, he admits that he was a bit out of practice. Carrying a .318, he followed a big bull into some dense bush. He was close behind. Without warning the bull suddenly swapped ends and came rushing back over his tracks. The range was very close. Bell snapped a shot at him but missed the brain. He says that he just had time to jump aside and put another shot into the elephant's heart as the brute rushed over the very spot he had been standing on a moment before. The muzzle of his rifle was within inches of the elephant's side as he fired.

Now Bell was much too fine a marksman to miss an African elephant's head at 10 yards' range; yet the elephant took not the slightest notice of the shot--a heavy bullet would have brought him to his knees. Then Bell's luck stood him in good stead by permitting this to take place in a type of bush which allowed him to jump to one side out of the elephant's way. But I know places, and I don't doubt Bell knows similar ones, in which the resilience of the bush would merely throw you back under the elephant's feet. It's a moot point whether being trampled underfoot by an elephant would be preferable to impalement on a tusk! I have no hankering to experience either.

Since I have repeatedly urged both orally and in print that no light bullet can possibly stun an African elephant if it misses the brain even by but a small amount (owing to the honeycomb formation of his skull, which dissipates the bullets' punch), and that only a heavy slug can hit a sufficiently powerful blow to have it transmitted to the brain, the question is certain to be asked: How do I account for the indubitable fact that Bell stunned many elephant with both 7mm and .303 rifles? And as any truly experienced hunter can tell instantly that Bell belongs to that select few-- and all too few they are--who have put on paper their African hunting experiences and told us the truth and nothing but the truth, without allowing their imaginations to run away with them to the extent of inserting fictional adventures and observations for the benefit of the thrill lovers, there can be no doubt whatever of the accuracy of his descriptions. For instance, there was the occasion when he dropped a mighty tusker and climbed up on his back for reconnaissance while his man cut off the tail. Bell then jumped down and went on to kill a number of other tuskers, but after he had left that first big one recovered consciousness, got to his feet, and cleared off minus his tail without anyone's being the wiser until they failed to find him next day, although the mark where he fell was plainly to be seen. There can be no question that elephant was truly stunned, knocked out--yet the rifle was a 7mm and the bullet only weighed 173 grains.

My answer is that Bell did not miss the brain; the elephant was not stunned by "having the bullet pass close to the brain," as Bell says. I contend that the bullet just lacked the necessary momentum to carry it on into one of the more vital regions. If this is admitted there would be no question of the shock being transmitted to the brain for the excellent reason that it would have been administered to the actual brain itself, where a very slight tap would be sufficient to stun even an African elephant.

# 15

# LIONS DON'T COME EASY

## By Jack O'Connor

### Outdoor Life, November 1953

*It is my hope that someday I will be able to sit in front of a campfire in Africa, sip a sundowner and listen to a lion roar in the darkness. No other animal epitomizes a safari in Africa more than the lion. He's called King Of The Beasts, but most professional hunters claim that he hasn't earned the title. A good-size male lion will still weigh 400 to 500 pounds, however, and that's a lot of cat to contend with if you get him mad at you.*

*John Kingsley-Heath, a professional hunter whose name appears elsewhere in this book, guided Jack O'Connor on a safari in 1959. Two years later, Kingsley-Heath, while protecting a client, was terribly mangled by a lion. The lion is a true Africa heavyweight.*

P ractically everyone who has never hunted in Africa will assure you that there is nothing to getting a lion. All you have to do, they say, is drive around in a safari car for a few hours, looking over various samples of the king of beasts. Then, when you find the kind you want, one with a mane that exactly matches the pine paneling in the rumpus room, you just step out and give him the business.

Yet I have just finished eight days of dawn-to-dark hunting--and only this morning did I shoot my lion. Incidentally, I shot the seventy-eighth lion I saw--an average of almost 10 a day. There are still plenty of them in the best areas of British East Africa, but unless you are lucky you have to rustle to get a good one.

The three of us--H. W. (Herb) Klein, M. C. (Red) Early, and I-- first started to think about a lion hunt back in 1950, when we were chasing Dall sheep and grizzlies in the Yukon. Herb and Red, old friends of mine, like to hunt and shoot and fondle a firearm as much as I do. Both are husky Texas oil men, and they have hunted everything from Texas white-tail deer to Alaska brown bear. They are among the half-dozen hunters who have taken all varieties of North American wild sheep. When you've accomplished things like that, you have to begin to raise your sights a bit.

One night we were gabbing in our Yukon cook tent when Herb suddenly said, "What do you say we take a whirl at lions in Africa one of these days?"

"Sounds good to me," Red grunted.

I said little, but all my life I had, like most American sportsmen, dreamed of the fabulous game country that is East Africa--of the great, black, truculent Cape buffalo; the fantastic wildebeest, which looks like a cross between a mule, a deer, and a buffalo; the leopard; the elephant; the many strange antelope. But most of all I had dreamed of someday knocking over a great-maned lion, the grandest of the cats, the epitome of all that is Africa.

The dream began to come true last fall, when "Outdoor Life" gave me the go-ahead on the trip. The three of us engaged the famous Nairobi outfitting firm of Ker & Downey Safaris, Ltd., and for months we were busy getting together rifles, ammunition, and photographic equipment, obtaining passports, and enduring injections for everything from cholera to housemaid's knee. Stories of the Mau Mau trouble gave us pause, but we discovered that the uprisings were confined to an area far from the hunting fields. Finally last June we met in New York and flew to Nairobi by way of London, Paris, Rome, and Khartoum in the Sudan.

Three and a half days out of Nairobi we were in our first hunting camp in northwestern Tanganyika with Don Ker and Myles Turner, white hunters, 26 native helpers--gunbearers, cooks, drivers--and two hunting cars and two big five-ton trucks. The camping equipment would knock your eye out. Nairobi outfitters cater to the carriage trade, and while we hunt we live in style.

As I write this, I am sitting at a portable typewriter in a clean, airy, and spacious dining tent. While I labor at one end of the table, Don Ker and Red Early are playing blackjack at the other. Herb

Klein has just come in with a zebra and a Thomson's gazelle. Hot and tired after stalking the zebra, he is taking a bath in a folding canvas tub while his personal boy stands by with the towels. This is astonishing luxury for an old desert rat like me, who on most of his trips has been his own guide, his own cook, and his own skinner.

The amount of game we've seen has been fantastic. I have hunted from Mexico to Alaska, but in the 12 days since we left Nairobi I have seen more game than ever before. Yesterday we saw at least 10,000 zebras. Beautiful little Thomson's gazelles hop around in the tall grass like so many fleas; we've surely seen over a million of them. And hundreds of giraffes and ostriches; thousands of topi, wildebeests, and goofy-looking kongoni.

Game of some sort is continually in sight. Here you see a herd of gazelles, over there you see a few water bucks among the trees. Beyond the hill a zebra barks like a cocky little dog, and a dainty dik-dik, an antelope no larger than a rabbit, scurries through the grass.

The same armchair hunter who tells you that catching your lion is easy, also tells you that Africa is hot. Of course it is. That's why, when an acquaintance back in the States advised me to take an eiderdown jacket for early-morning wear, I thought he was balmy. But I took it along--and it's the most useful garment I have. We've been camping at about 5,000 feet. Nights are so cool we sleep under two or three blankets. And in the morning my jacket is as welcome as it was in the Yukon.

But back to the lions. We made our first camp near a donga, or dry stream bed. Tents were being set up when Myles called to Herb and me. "Come here, pals," he said. "I want to show you something."

In the mud beside a nearby water hole were the big round pug marks of two lions, "A lion and a lioness," Myles told us. "This look good!"

Actually they were even better than we had hoped.

After lunch we went out in the hunting cars, Myles with Herb and Red, and Don Ker taking me. We were not a mile from camp when Don suddenly put on the brakes. "See the lions?" he asked, lifting his binoculars to his eyes.

I jumped as if I had been shot, but I managed to follow the direction of his gaze. Across the donga, perhaps 150 yards away, and beneath a big thorn tree, were the silhouettes of a couple of lions. They looked just like the circus kind. Then my binoculars showed me lions all over the place--females, half-grown cubs, and a couple of young males with sprouting manes.

For whatever the reason, lions are not afraid of automobiles. Putting his four-wheel-drive hunting car into low, Don crossed the donga and in a moment we were up to our necks in lions. Those around the thorn tree posed like mama, papa, and the children in an old-fashioned family portrait. More lions popped up out of the grass until there were 18 in all.

Breaking out my black-and-white still camera, I shot several pictures of them. Then I turned to color movies. One lithe and beautiful young lioness detached herself from the group, walked up to within a few feet of the car, and looked it over.

Reluctantly we drove away. This, I told myself, was going to be a cinch. I was even more convinced we were on the gravy train when we saw two more lionesses, shortly after. They were lying in the thin shade of a thorn tree right out on the hot, bright plain. One was devouring the carcass of a Thomson's gazelle she had killed, and when we drew up and stopped she nervously picked up the dead Tommy and trotted away until she found herself another tree. She didn't know what the strange mechanical monster was, but she wasn't going to share her Tommy with it, that was sure.

That same afternoon I shot my first African game--a Tommy for us dudes and the white hunters to gnaw on, and a topi for the help. Each was a one-shot kill with an 87-grain bullet from the .257 Weatherby Magnum, and each was made at around 200 yards.

I figured I'd really have something to tell Herb and Red when I got back. I had actually seen some real live lions with hair, long teeth, and big red mouths. I had also actually shot a couple of funny-looking un-American antelope. Would the boys be burning with envy?

But when Don and I drove up to camp my small accomplishments faded into nothing, for there was Red gloating over the carcass of a big blond lion, while the native boys whooped and hollered around him in triumph. Just as the debunkers had said; there's nothing to shooting a lion in Africa. You simply drive around until you see the one you want.

Actually, Red had done just that. From a distance Myles had spotted a lion and lioness lying in the grass. Leaving the car half a mile away, the two men had made a long stalk, creeping along on their hands and knees through the tall grass until they were about 75 yards from the lions. Then Red eased himself up onto the convenient anthill, and when the lion raised its head above the grass he plugged it through the neck.

Easy? For him, yes. But Herb and I didn't shoot our lions the next day, nor the day after that. We didn't shoot any old he-lions on account of we didn't see any. We saw lady lions. We saw baby lions. We even saw young legal males which we passed up because they had small manes.

In East Africa, male antelope (which by all laws of logic should be called bucks) are called rams if they are small and bulls if they are large, and the very feline male leopards and cheetahs are called dogs. So Herb and I gagged up our reports to each other when we met at night. "Oh, the usual! Lots of ewe and lamb lions, but no old boar lions."

We went out at dawn, came in after dark. We covered country in the hunting cars. We glassed from the little rocky hills called kopjes and pronounced "copies." We explored dongas. We shot a few antelope to keep our help sleek and fat and our own bodies and souls together. But what we wanted was a lion apiece.

I got the first break. We moved part of the outfit a few miles from the place where Red had shot his lion and camped on a donga spotted with water holes every half mile or so. The area was very dry and the high grass had been cured by the sun. All around us was the fresh, clean, delicious smell of natural hay.

A little scouting soon showed that the lions in the area were concentrated along this donga. They had cover in the brush along the watercourse, pools in which to drink, and plentiful game close at hand. Every night we could hear their grunting, coughing roars as they hunted. Water bucks, Thomson's gazelles, topi, impalas-- all came down to water and paid their toll to the great lurking cats.

There are various ways of getting lions. One is to cruise around in a hunting car until a shootable specimen is spotted and then to stalk him afoot. In both Kenya and Tanganyika the law says that no game may be shot from a car or within 200 yards of a car. So even if you spot a fine trophy lion you have to drive on at least 200 yards before you can get out and begin your stalk.

Another way is to hit fresh spoor, or tracks, follow the lion to his lair, boot him out, and take your shot at him. Still another is baiting. You shoot one of the commoner antelope and drag it behind an automobile to leave a blood-scent trail. Then you tie the bait animal securely in a tree so that a feeding lion cannot drag it off into the brush. Perhaps a shootable lion will be attracted to the bait, and still be there when you come around at daylight. But more often the bait has been devoured by other visitors-- buzzards, marabou storks, and hyenas. And when lions do come they are likely to be females and immature males that are not so wary of ambushes as the great maned lords of the jungle.

Don Ker elected to cruise in his hunting car, and we covered a beat along the donga, stopping now and then to glass our surroundings or to get out to look for sign. We saw lions every day-- sometimes a lone and beautiful female shining like gold in the early-morning sun as she lay full of antelope, replete, and happy, enjoying the warmth after the chill of the night at almost 6,000 feet. Sometimes we'd see two or three females or young lions together. Now and then they'd be sunning themselves, but in the afternoon they'd either be lying in the tall grass or bedded down in the thin shade of a thorn tree.

There were big he-lions about, no doubt of it. We'd see their tracks by the water holes. At night we'd hear their rattling low-pitched grunts, their full-throated, deep-chested roars. But when we went out at dawn they had gone back to their brush retreats. But sometime, somewhere, we'd be bound to see a trophy lion.

Then it happened.

One morning, just as the first clean, bright rays of the sun shone on bush and grassland, the lookout boy--his head through a hole in the car top--whispered that magic word, "Simba!" Across the donga, about 200 yards away, seated majestically on a big flat rock, were two big males, with a black and a blond mane respectively. My heart almost jumped out of my throat.

Calmly Don Ker, that old pro, stopped the hunting car, lifted his 7X35 Bausch & Lomb binoculars to his eyes, and took a look at the lions. "They're both worth shooting," he said calmly.

He drove on and parked the car some 300 yards away. Then Mr. O'Connor's personal whammy took a hand.

"Give me my three hundred," I told the gunbearer in the backseat.

That Weatherby Magnum is one of my favorites, a rifle I have described in these pages. It's a short-barreled, scope-sighted featherweight, so accurate it will keep five shots on a silver dollar at 200 yards.

So off we went. We dropped into the donga and presently came to a spot where I could shoot. The lions had become nervous.

Apparently they had seen or heard us because when I sat down to shoot, they were on their feet.

The rifle was wobbling all over the place. My first shot at the black-maned lion got away from me. I missed, and off went the old boy into the bush. I worked the bolt rapidly, then swung over to the blond. This time the crosshairs settled down right behind his shoulder, and when I squeezed off the shot I expected old Leo africanus to drop. Instead he gave no sign of being hit, turned his big broad fanny to me, slowly walked off the rock, and disappeared.

The only thing that could have happened, I told myself, was that I'd given the trigger a terrific yank and jerked my shot high.

As we sneaked back to the car I was about as low as I have been in all my life. I had dreamed for 40 years of killing a great-maned lion. Two of them had been tossed into my lap--and I had flubbed the opportunity like an excited schoolboy missing his first buck. I crept along trying to hide my head in my jacket. The gunbearers wouldn't look at me, and until we got into the car Don said not a word.

Then he turned to me. "Don't feel badly," he said. "Lots of people have missed their first lion --and they have missed at a lot less than 100 yards."

I said nothing. There was nothing to say. So off we drove. Presently Don stopped the car.

"We'll have to try baiting now," he told me. "See that kongoni over there, about 300 yards away? I'd like to have you shoot it."

The kongoni is a big, horse-faced antelope with short, twisted, cowlike horns and a gallop like that of a spavined plowhorse. Nobody loves the poor kongoni. He exists in multitudes but he isn't much of a trophy, and his destiny seems to be lion food and lion bait. This one stood under a tree asleep on his feet and with his head down. He was about 300 yards away and the shot should not be difficult with my souped-up .300 Magnum.

I held onto the tree with my left hand, rested the fore end of the .300 over my wrist, put the crosshairs on the center of the kongoni's shoulder, and touched one off. Not a darned thing happened except that--far away, through an avenue in the trees--I saw dust kick up. I felt even lower. I worked the bolt, squeezed off another careful shot with exactly the same result.

"Way high!" Don said gloomily.

"I'll try a 220-grain bullet," I said. "It shoots a lot lower."

I fed one in, held as before, shot, and down went the kongoni.

A great light dawned on me. Carefully I examined my .300. The continual pounding of the hunting car over rough country had loosened the guard screws of the rifle so that it took three complete turns to tighten them. The scope mount was so loose that I could rattle it with my hand. I tried a shot at 100 yards, and the bullet landed to the right and a foot high. Even the three screws in the scope base were loose. I had to remove the scope to tighten them, and the .300, of course, was out of action until I could sight it in again. I didn't have a lion, but I did have an alibi.

In the rack in the hunting car was my .375 Magnum, a Model 70 Winchester restocked by Griffin & Howe and fitted with a Stith 2 3/4X on a Griffin & Howe mount. I took it out, tightened the guard screws, then shot twice with the 270-grain bullet at a knot on a tree 100 paces away. One shot was in the middle of the knot, the other about one inch away. Here was my lion rifle.

I got another chance a couple of days later. We were cruising along early one morning when what should we behold about 200 yards away but two big blond lions strolling along as amiable-looking as two well-fed house cats, their big bellies--full of meat and water--swinging from side to side as they walked.

It would have been very easy to leap from the hunting car with cries of joy and to salivate, but the Tanganyika game laws and the long arm of Don Ker's conscience would not permit. We cruised slowly between them, as if shooting lions was the last thing in the world we'd think of. I even thrust my camera out of the car and shot a picture of one.

But when we got about a quarter mile away we grabbed rifles, dived into the donga, and ran like the devil after the lions. When we got to the spot where they should be, we stuck our heads over the bank expecting to see them. No lions. Their tracks showed they had done exactly what we had done. As soon as they were out of sight they had run.

So we took up the spoor. For five miles we followed it, with Don, the gunbearer Thomas, and a Wandorobo tracker doing most of the work. I must say with pride, though, that two or three times I found the spoor when it was lost.

It was noon. We were hot, weary, and thirsty when we saw a little Thomson's gazelle standing just out of a brush patch into which the tracks led, and gazing at something the way a bird looks at a snake.

"He sees the lions," Don hissed at me. "Get ready!"

So into the brush we crept. But the lions saw us first and we became aware of them as bouncing silhouettes fleeing through heavy brush about 75 yards away. I brought up the .375 and had the crosshairs swinging along the chest of a lion when Don shouted for me not to shoot. Like all white hunters he wants no part of a wounded lion in heavy brush.

We chased the cats about 300 yards and saw them again across an open flat just before they disappeared into another brush patch.

"Shoot if you think you can land one right!" Don yelled.

"Hell, I couldn't hit an elephant right now," I said as I gasped for breath.

So back we turned, again defeated. We had now spooked four big-maned lions and we were really loused up.

The next day, not far from where we lost those two, Herb Klein polished off a big blond male, probably one of the two we had muffed. Don and I continued to see lady lions but no males.

So back we went to our first camp, where Red had shot his lion. We held a conference and decided to try two more days for my lion. Since Herb and Red had killed not only lions but leopards-- something for which I had no license-i was time to move on to other territory for other game.

The next morning we saw a big pride of 18 lions, including two young maned males. The temptation to bop one was pretty strong. That afternoon we put out a kongoni bait and chopped in two a big eland which Herb had shot the day before.

It was gray dawn the second day when Don and I drove out in the hunting car to inspect our three baits. When we could see the first one Don said calmly, "There's something on the kongoni--a lioness, I believe." He lifted his glasses. "No, it's a lion."

My own binoculars went to my eyes. I saw a very respectable maned male, young but shootable and a better lion than most Americans come back from Africa with. "I'll settle for that baby," I said.

Don kept the glass to his eyes.

"We've got two more baits to look at," he told me, "and I'd hate to have you go back with a second-rate lion like that one."

"You wouldn't hate it half as much as I'd hate to go back without any lion," I told him. "My best friends wouldn't speak to me."

"Well, maybe he'll be here when we get back," he said.

"You're the doctor!"

Off we went. The second bait had not been touched, but when we got to the third we could see that a lion had been eating on it and below it in the dust were the big round tracks of a male.

We parked the car away from the kill and got out. "He hasn't been gone from the bait for more than a few minutes," Don whispered. "He's bound to be close by."

We had hardly gone 300 yards through the tall grass and thin brush when the Wandorobo boy whispered, "Simba!"

Now luck was with us. A bit less than a hundred yards from the lion was a big anthill that would give us cover from the stalk and a rest to shoot from. Slowly, quietly, hardly daring to breathe, we crept up on his nibs. I poked my head over the hill. There was the great lion. He was sitting in grass so tall that only his head and neck showed, nervously looking in the direction of his free meal, half of Herb's bull eland. His shaggy, majestic head and thick mane shone golden in the early-morning sun.

Cautiously I poked the big .375 over the top of the anthill. I rested the fore end on my left hand and the crosshair in the scope came to rest rock-steady against his burly neck. I squeezed the trigger so gradually that the rifle seemed to go off by itself.

As the 71.5 grains of No. 4064 powder exploded and drove the 270-grain soft-point bullet into the great cat's neck, all hell broke loose. Roaring like a fiend possessed, the lion tossed his great tawny body clear of the grass in his dying convulsions. I have heard many a wounded grizzly roar in his death agonies, and it's a blood-curdling sound, but I have never heard more racket than that big lion made.

We rushed forward for the finishing shots, and I was so excited that if Don hadn't restrained me, I think I would have tried to stab him to death with my pocketknife.

We stood over him. We gloated. We measured. We admired. He was a beautiful lion. His great sandy body was as smooth and round as a sausage. His blond mane was heavy, shaggy, long. Don Ker told me he probably weighed 500 pounds, and was one of the largest lions he had seen in 27 years as a white hunter. From the tip of his nose to the last joint of his tail he was nine feet, seven inches long as he lay there.

All in all, he was some lion, and of all the trophies I have taken, the only one that has given me a greater thrill was the first desert ram I stood over, almost a quarter of a century earlier and half a world away.